Ethics,
Excellence,
and Economics

Keys to
Entrepreneurial
Development

by
Tommy Reid

ELIM
EP
PUBLISHING

Elim Publishing, Inc.
Lima, New York

Ethics, Excellence, and Economics
Key to Entrepreneurial Development
ISBN 1-59919-001-X
Copyright © 1989, 2005 by Tommy Reid
P.O. Box 590
Orchard Park, New York 14127

Republished by Elim Publishing
1679 Dalton Road
Lima, NY 14485

Original ISBN 0-89274-534-7
Published by Honor Books
A Division of Harrison House
P.O. Box 35035
Tulsa, Oklahoma 74153

Ethics, Excellence, and Economics

Keys to Entrepreneurial Development

Additional copies of
Ethics, Excellence and Economics
are available at your local bookstore
or by contacting:

Elim Publishing
1679 Dalton Road
Lima, New York 14485

www.elimpublishing.com
info@elimpublishing.com

To my friend,
Dr. Ken Lipke,
a man of faith and integrity

Contents

Foreword by Oral Roberts
Tulsa, Oklahoma

The Christian business ethics of Michael Cardone Sr. and Michael Cardone Jr. are, to my knowledge, so close to the Bible in their day-by-day application that I am honored to see them referred to in this book.

The chapter on *The Premise* is of special interest to me, and I appreciate it. I am praying that the entire book will inspire all of us to an actual walk with God, Who is not only our God and our Source but is the greatest businessperson of all.

Foreword by Paul Yonggi Cho

Yoido Full Gospel Church
Seoul, Korea

Disillusionment and shattered dreams come to many of us in this life, but there is nothing quite so shattering as a business or an entire industry failing. "Could it have been avoided?" is always a question asked in such situations. Dr. Tommy Reid has carefully viewed these failures, felt the needs of the people who were affected when they lost their jobs, and checked to see if the goals and visions of those who failed were grounded in the Word of God. Goals built upon Bible principles still work in industry and for the people associated with those industries whether the people are Christian or not. "Rulership or leadership must be from a servant's throne," Dr. Reid said.

Too often even Christians claim high morals and ethics within the church and among Christian friends, but this same standard is divorced from all business dealings in order to maintain an image of development and growth outside of the church. In this book, the emphasis is on Biblical principles that were characteristic of the widespread and rapid growth of the United States, principles that caused the nation to forge ahead through all kinds of difficulty, and that can help it to revive industries again.

Where there is life, there is a ray of hope that renewal, reformation, and restoration can come again. The strong artery of any industry or people can receive a new infusion of life from searching out these principles and beginning to live by them.

Dr. Reid's sensitive insights on the frightening situation that occurred in Buffalo, New York, and his many hours of counseling, inquiring, and searching for answers has brought this book into being.

A wealth of knowledge and principles are discussed, and the reader will be greatly blessed and benefitted as he prayerfully considers — and then practices — them. I heartily endorse this book.

Thoughts from a:

Church Leader

According to the purposes of God in any generation, He raises men as spokesmen to address specific areas of need in people's lives. No messenger in the contemporary Church brings more insight into Christian standards demonstrated in the work place than Pastor Tommy Reid. The message of *Ethics, Excellence, and Economics* challenges Christians to activate spiritual ideals in everyday experiences. The vision moves Christians beyond the sanction of church walls and stained-glass windows to impact the world.

Jesus described an unseen Kingdom to those who "had ears to hear." He offered people standards of quality living in this world that were simple, practical, and most importantly, attainable. Christians never have the right to separate the sacred from the secular in any situations of human interaction. The world is our harvest field. Separation from the world cuts off our witness to it. In a self-seeking society, spiritual qualities of compassion, faithfulness, discipline, and honesty not only develop best in our common, daily tasks, but they also shine as a light of witness to others. As we abide in Christ, we are called to influence and infiltrate the world with a life-changing message.

At the same time, a Christian's work is his proving ground, the place to test the work of the Holy Spirit within us as we grow and produce fruit which is eternal. Work pressures alert Christians to the spiritual areas where they need to mature in relationships as well as productivity. No other setting provides more opportunities for spiritual growth than the work place. We have a critical responsibility to "live what we say" as an eternally deciding factor in the lives of those who read the Gospel of Christ in us.

Tommy Reid has simplified the complexities of problems in business and industry with a focus on servanthood, excellence, and God-given creativity. The multi-faceted problems threatening the world's markets become the entree' to introduce solutions found only in God's wisdom. Christians become the "Daniels" and "Josephs" of our generation. All good things come from God. In a day of unemployment, layoffs, cutbacks, a tottering economy, and unpredictable stock market swings, the Gospel of peace and hope for the future is indeed "good news."

Tommy Reid's answers are not "pie in the sky" promises intended to placate 20th century anxieties. Instead, he calls for us to take responsibility for our world by living out the most fundamental mandates which Jesus gave to those who follow Him. The Kingdom of God will not come in observation, but in the demonstration of eternal truth by the power of the Holy Spirit within us. We must not back away from a bold declaration of God's will, even though principles of righteousness, peace and joy seem at times to go against an overwhelming tide of despair.

Christians cannot close their eyes to social oppression. Too often, we become inoculated to racism, inequity, and abuse that surround us. Individually, we dare not ignore the numerous warnings of accountability to God for the quality and diligence of our work and our responsibility for the welfare of co-workers. We must carefully guard our own hearts from the subtle traps of Mammon that corrupt our motivation for productivity. We need keen discernment in these daily situations which Tommy Reid alerts us to recognize.

Jesus came to lift us to a dimension of quality living. He lived as the firstfruit of a new way of thinking, relating, and behaving in our world. Jesus set the standard for us as the perfect example of Kingdom values. He taught us that God is vitally interested in the quality and choices of our lives, as well as in the outward demonstration of our inner convictions.

The manifestation of the Kingdom of God depends upon Christians realizing their responsibility to live as Kingdom "leaven" in the midst of a society wallowing in corruption. As darkness covers the earth, this is the generation of an emerging, glorious Church, a bride without spot or wrinkle, a city set upon a hill. Where is a more obvious place for that bright "City" to shine her light to those in darkness than in the kingdoms of business and industry? Where is the opportunity greater? Where is the challenge more necessary for our survival?

Without proposing a formula to which we could give intellectual assent and then forget, Tommy Reid's insights tap our sensitivity to see our work with enduring spiritual vision. He says that perhaps the life and need for this book will be short if we join together in the restoration and rebuilding of foundational spiritual truths toward our work. As one who believes that we are in a time of pressing toward the Kingdom of God as no other generation in history, I agree with the author's plea for urgency in implementation! God has spoken a vision and direction through His messenger. Now the responsibility and rewards for carrying out that vision rest with those who have ears to hear what the Spirit is saying to the Church!

Foreword by Bishop John L. Meares

Evangel Temple
Washington, D.C.

To know Pastor Tommy Reid as a friend is comforting, and to learn of the principles by which he has lived and achieved is to be challenged. To feel his heartbeat is compelling and motivating to bring about progressive change.

I first met Tommy Reid in the late Fifties while involved in a revival crusade in Hong Kong, that great city often referred to as the crossroads of the world. He was the founding pastor of the church that was gathered together as a result of that crusade. Under his ministry and administration, the church became an influence that continues today in the very heart of that great metropolitan city.

Following his ministry in Hong Kong, he became assistant pastor to Paul Yonggi Cho in the church that was to become world-renowned. Yoido Full Gospel Church of Seoul, Korea, now is the largest church in the world with a membership of more than half a million people.

Tommy Reid has practiced the principles carefully outlined in this book through many years of productive ministry; however, they have been exemplified best in his upper New York State ministry.

In 1963, he accepted the pastorate of a small, unnoticed church in Buffalo, New York. Under his leadership, the Full Gospel Tabernacle of Buffalo has grown to an active membership of more than four thousand. This thriving church has mothered and established five other strong churches in the area with an additional membership of more than eight thousand. Internationally, he has been active in planting churches in several countries, particularly in the Far East.

The impact of his ministry has contributed both to the spiritual and the economic well-being of people in an area considered one of the most economically depressed in our nation. The name "Pastor Tommy Reid" is recognized immediately in leadership and pastoral conferences throughout this nation and abroad. His agenda is filled with invitations as a principal speaker among religious leaders throughout the world.

He firmly believes that "to him who is spiritual, all things are spiritual." Therefore, the principles taught by Jesus must be applied in the community, in the marketplace, and in every area of our lives in order to accomplish a renewal of our society.

In this book, you will feel the warmth of his concern as you are confronted with his conviction for change in one's self with the radiant hope of together changing our world. This book is a must for every person who truly seeks for success and fulfillment for one's self and others. Its message is vitally important to this generation.

The Problem

Men groan from out of the city,
and the soul of the wounded crieth out . . . .
Job 24:12

The Promise

For there is hope of a tree, if it be cut down,
that it will sprout again,
and that the tender branch thereof will not cease.

Though the root thereof wax old in the earth,
and the stock thereof die in the ground;

Yet through the scent of water it will bud,
and bring forth boughs like a plant.

Job 14:7-9

The Premise

If my people, which are called by my name,
shall humble themselves, and pray,
and seek my face, and turn from their wicked ways;
then will I hear from heaven,
and will forgive their sin,
and will heal their land.

2 Chronicles 7:14

Renewal Through Recommitment and Reformation:
The Message and the Model

1
The Message:
God's Principles for Industry

Certainly religious leaders already have addressed the problems of our new society, but too few seem to have any sense of genuine hope for the future survival of industrial America. But there is a ray of hope, and a plan can be developed not only for industrial survival but for the renaissance of American business. As a pragmatic pastor, I hear the Word of the Lord saying:

> . . . **The kingdoms of this world are become the kingdoms of our Lord, and of his Christ; and he shall reign for ever and ever.**
>
> **Revelation 11:15**

I believe it will happen. Kingdoms rise and fall as presidents and kings are replaced, die, or are deposed. Real and raw power lies in the business community. Even if administrations and governments change, industrialists, bankers, and entrepreneurs spell the difference between successes and failures of any country's economics. Wars almost always are fought for economic reasons. Real earthly power resides in the hands of those who control economic destiny. Solomon admitted this, saying, . . . **money answereth all things** (Eccl. 10:19).

The kingdoms of this world, I believe, are industries such as General Motors, IBM, Exxon, and so forth, and if industry is to survive, all those kingdoms must come under the control and influence of a "servant-throne" mentality. Jesus clearly taught that real rulership and leadership must be from a servant's throne.

A Look at Industry

"The good news is the bad news is wrong," according to Ben J. Wattenberg in his challenging book by the same title. He boldly states the audio recording in a 1984 Chrysler, "All monitored systems are functioning normally," could have been the title of his incisive book and strongly suggests the current pessimism in the business community is unfounded in fact. Wattenberg says we should look more at possibilities than at perceived problems, and the future holds more promise than many believe.[1] I agree.

The Problem

Admittedly there are many things wrong with industry in the nations of North America. But things are far from hopeless. It is possible to do something about these problems. That is what this book is all about. There is a ray of hope that we can see, and renewal, reformation, and restoration *can* come to these countries.

Not long ago, I read the best-selling book, *In Search of Excellence: Lessons From America's Best-Run Companies* by Peters and Waterman. I was struck by how practical the principles cited are in exemplifying excellence in

---

[1]Ben Wattenberg, *The Good News Is the Bad News Is Wrong* (New York: Simon and Schuster, 1984).

corporations. The authors tout their tome as the "good news" for American business. They say:

> The findings from the excellent companies amount to an upbeat message. There is good news for America. Good management practice today is not resident only in Japan. But, more important, the good news comes from treating people decently and asking them to shine, and from producing things that work.[2]

Those four sentences could serve as the text for a sermon. Jesus said:

> **And as ye would that men should do to you, do ye also to them likewise.**
>
> **Luke 6:31**

I have found that the Sermon on the Mount provides guidance for the individual Christian life, but also serves as a more detailed exposition of the Golden Rule and outlines principles for good business practices and business ethics. The "Good News" for industry — both labor and management — is outlined carefully in the Bible through both commandment and example.

The Bible as Guide

The Bible can serve as an excellent *guide* for any businessman, but it must be the *standard* for the Christian businessman. The mandate is clear, and excellence for a Christian life and a Christian business is stated succinctly.

---

[2]Copyright © 1982 by Thomas J. Peters and Robert H. Waterman Jr. Reprinted by permission from *In Search of Excellence* by Harper & Row, Publishers, Inc.

> **Be ye therefore perfect, even as your Father which is in heaven is perfect.**
>
> **Matthew 5:48**

However, this book is more than a call to Christian businesspersons. I believe the Bible can and will speak to all who are deeply interested in solving the pressing problems of today. In any kind of business, at every level there is a standard for owners, presidents, managers, secretaries, janitors, pressmen, drivers, carpenters, painters, clerks, line workers — every person, whether employee or employer. And this standard is the message of my book.

The Message Versus Reality

Sadly, what should be and what is very often are different.

What *should* happen is for Christians at all levels of business and industry to put into practice Christ's principles as revealed in Scripture and thereby to influence and inspire employers and other co-workers. There is an amazing fact about Bible principles: Because of the infinite grace of God, one does not have to be a believer to benefit from their practice. Biblical principles work and work well. Thus, even the most adamant unbeliever still would find it worthwhile to consider Bible principles of business carefully.

Only a fool would ignore the greatest single collection of distilled wisdom the world has known. I have found those wisest of words from the Blessed Book to keep me from "reinventing the wheel" and from repeating mistakes from history.

With this in mind, we come to an important question: What is really happening in American business and industry?

Is everything really as "upbeat" as Peters and Waterman suggest? Are the excellent companies typical of American business? And are they really "excellent?"

For nearly three decades I have watched my city of Buffalo, New York, suffer while locked in a life-and-death battle against the cancer of unemployment. As a pastor, I have buried those destroyed in the battle. I have tried to help the disillusioned put back together their fractured and fragmented dreams. I have labored hard to hold out hope and to nurture the bruised, broken, and struggling souls of my community. While I am by nature a dreamer, a visionary, my dreams and visions have been tempered by living through the long, black night of human suffering and despair. Also, I pray these dreams and visions are grounded solidly in the life-giving Word of God.

My dream is to bring the message of what *should* be to those suffering from what *is* and transform a dark reality into a bright hope.

Problems in Buffalo — Grain and Steel

The first disaster that crippled Buffalo's working class was the demise of the mammoth grain industries that had fed our city for many decades. A boat ride on the Buffalo River reveals dozens of empty, weather-ravaged grain silos, crumbling from disrepair and disuse. Yet, while the demise of the local grain industry was crippling, it was not totally devastating in its impact. Another industry rose to take up the slack.

Buffalo recovered from the brink of ruin, resuscitated by the burgeoning new steel industry. Soon the giant, sprawling mills, glowing with fire and booming with noise, spread along the riverbanks overshadowing the empty and dead grain silos. It was an answer to prayer as more and more people found employment, prosperity — and they believed — security in steel. The steelworkers virtually gave their lives to the industry.

But then, slowly, decay set in. Reports and rumors of a flagging steel market spread. Fingers of blame and shame were pointed in all directions — greedy management, labor union demands, foreign competition, the need to modernize, and on and on. Rumors, although denied at times, began to turn into realities. The mills cut back dramatically in production, resulting in hundreds being laid off. Soon whole sections were shut down and the army of unemployed bloated to thousands. Finally, entire mills were mothballed and virtually abandoned. There was a growing sense of panic and hopelessness in Buffalo.

Now joining the crumbling grain silos, empty mills covering innumerable acres stand decaying, dead, or dying.

The Walking Wounded

Unemployment devastates a community more tragically and in different ways than an earthquake or other natural disasters. When a tornado or a flood occurs, the disaster comes and goes, and rebuilding can follow. Restoring buildings and replacing material possessions is expensive, but we know how to deal with such a passing tragedy. However, unemployment lingers and grows like a cancer in society. As months and years pass, more and more are claimed by the disease in its natural progression through cause and effect. No business or individual is left untouched. And few know how to deal with the problem. It seems too big and too complicated to be solved, because unemployment goes beyond simply "not having an income."

John C. Raines, associate professor at Temple University in Philadelphia, clearly links unemployment to severe social problems.[3] His studies reveal that for every 1 percent increase in sustained unemployment there is a 6 percent increase in homicides among young men between the ages of 15 and 24. Admissions to mental hospitals increase 3 percent among women and 5 percent among men. In addition, he observed marked increases in alcohol and drug abuse, family violence, suicides, and divorces precipitated by unemployment. The personal tragedy of devalued self-image, repeated rejections, and intense financial pressures added to all other elements are simply more than some can handle.

The Responsibility of the Church

Clearly we must address the continuing problem of unemployment and of closing businesses. The writer of Ecclesiastes observed:

> **In the day of prosperity be joyful, but in the day of adversity consider: God also hath set the one over against the other. . . .**

> **Ecclesiastes 7:14**

---

[3] John C. Raines, *Modern Work and Human Meaning* (Philadelphia: Westminster, 1986).

31

Times for many are bad. Therefore, we must "consider" and recognize there are lessons we can learn during these difficult days, principles we can apply, goals we can redirect. These times call for careful and prayerful thinking and action. We cannot simply stand by and let this tragedy continue.

Theologian-sociologist Gregory Baum takes issue with psychiatrists, psychologists, pastors, and counselors who too often merely encourage people to adjust to an unjust society rather than helping them confront wrongs and work through change. If Pharoah had had a team of psychiatrists in Egypt (during the captivity and Exodus), Baum questions whether he would have been able to tranquilize the people of Israel and whether they would have found life in Egypt more acceptable. Pointing to unemployment problems, Baum asks: Is it really enough to offer a therapy to the disturbed, unemployed person which merely helps him or her to calmly accept the tragedy?[4]

Perhaps another question would put the situation into better perspective: Did Christ just counsel the people to accept and endure the money-changers in the Temple, or did He take direct action to remove them?

While the answer is obvious, not so obvious is the answer to the problem of unemployment and difficulties of industry. However, I believe there *is* an answer, a ray of hope, and it includes both principles and practice.

---

[4]Gregory Baum, "Theology Questions Psychiatry: An Address," *The Ecumentist* 20:4, pp. 55-59.

For several years I had preached and proclaimed these principles from my pulpit at Full Gospel Tabernacle in Buffalo. But it seemed as if I needed a model to prove the principles. That is when an exceedingly bright and talented businessman came into my life, a man who had been taking these same principles — which he had learned on his own — and had been applying them in the rough and tumble world of the steel industry. His name is Dr. Ken Lipke, the owner of Gibraltar Steel Company.

Dr. Lipke and I have spent long hours together wrestling with the critical problems facing industry, particularly the steel industry, which to many, is a dinosaur on the verge of extinction. I have come away from these long sessions convinced there is hope and there are solutions within our grasp. There is much life left in the steel industry, as well as in other faltering American businesses.

Hope — Hi-Tech or Renewal?

Author Alvin Toffler taught Americans much about the effect of changing technology on institutions that we think are unchanging, such as education, culture, and even entertainment. His books, *Future Shock* and *The Third Wave*, are very prophetic in a secular sense.[5]

In the latter book, he claimed agriculture was the first wave of civilization, in which men survived by living off what they raised. Communities were built or broken by uncertain whims of weather. Rain or drought brought feast or famine.

---

[5]Alvin Toffler, *Future Shock* (New York: Random House, 1970); *The Third Wave* (New York: Bantam Books, 1981).

Toffler said the second wave was industry, which offered somewhat more security but wreaked havoc on the environment and the family structure.

Now, he warns us, we must prepare for the wash of the third wave, a super-technological revolution.

"Hi-tech" is the catchword of our times, and some push aside older "sunset" industries that carry the stigma of sweatshops, child labor, and violent labor-management conflicts. We are caught in a "crack in time" as the old and the new overlap. According to the experts, we must expect casualties in the change. Since change is inevitable, so is the damage it causes as the fabric of society is torn, caught in the ever-turning wheels of time. All we can do, they say, is to let time heal the wounds. I disagree. I believe there is a "third way" not just a "third wave."

While diagnosis is not cure, it is a step to health. We must know what is wrong in order to understand what needs to be corrected. However, we must go beyond this. This book is written from the perspective of a pastor, along with significant contributions from two successful industrialists. We examine the problems and hopefully offer real solutions.

Biblical Morality

Industry has begun to die because, I believe, too many businessmen have divorced Biblical morality and ethics from business. Corporate America must come back to an awareness that it is not only an economic entity responsible for production and distribution of goods but also a moral force. Thus, it must act and exist responsibly.

Toffler seems to agree with this premise. He says:

> Today's corporate critics attack the artificial divorce of economics from politics, morality, and other dimensions of life. A corporation is no longer responsible simply for making a profit or producing goods, but for simultaneously contributing to the solution of extremely complex ecological, moral, political, racial, sexual, and social problems.[6]

Greed

Perhaps corporate America has too many times violated these laws as set forth in Scripture, and that has caused the crisis in our country. Could it be that our motives of bringing goods and services to the consumer have too often given way to base motives of greed and lust? This perhaps led logically to an over-emphasis on short-term profits rather than long-term productivity.

Absentee Landlords

A second violation of scriptural principles also disturbs me. This is the serious moral infraction when huge areas of a city's real estate belong to "absentee landlords." This tends to lessen care for the preservation and prosperity of a local community.

I see a moral and economic renewal with creative entrepreneurship that can cause some of the sprawling, industrial complexes to be returned to local ownership. To some small extent this already has begun, but the trend must continue and expand to ensure economic

---

[6]*The Third Wave*, pp. 234,235.

recovery. Ownership must go hand-in-hand with care and concern for the community and its people.

True Wealth From the Ground

A third principle to keep in mind is that true wealth comes from the ground.

The ability of any nation to harvest and process the fruit of its soil is a direct result of our ability to harvest food products, mine ores, discover utilization of gas and oil, and recover other precious minerals from the ground.

Futurists often state that industry is doomed in America and that we have no choice but to become an "information/service-centered society," if we are to compete in a global economy. I disagree.

We must have, and must continue to develop, the ability to harvest and process the fruit of our ground even in this brave new world of ever-changing technology. The simple fact remains that the greatest consumer of "hi-tech" goods and services is America's industries.

National Security

We must not be mistaken: Even national security is at stake.

Every conflict in our history has been fought with weapons made of steel. If the current rate of demise continues in our steel mills, we will lose our ability to defend our lands. Today, we are almost as steel dependent as we were oil dependent in the 1970s. Something must be done to break the cycle. We cannot continue to be dependent on foreign steel, if we are to stay strong. International friends have a disturbing knack for changing into enemies overnight. The very nations we depend on for steel today easily could be our enemies tomorrow.

Models for Revival

Powerful models already exist in America that point the way to industrial renewal. In this book, I will introduce two of these models. The first is both in the man and in the industry he has built. This model is marked by servanthood toward the supplier, competitor, customer, and employee, and is it based on individual entrepreneurship and the participation of individual employees.

In the same way, the second model-industry uses as its motto, *Excellence in all things, and in all things, Glory to God*. Through an insistence on quality merchandise for the customer and an ever present concern for the hundreds of employees, the company has advanced in an unusual but highly competitive industry. With an incentive toward individual safety and production, it serves to uplift the employee while at the same time producing "zero defects" for the customers.

Perhaps the life of, and the need for, this book will be short. My prayer is that all of us will play our roles in the rebuilding of the industrial walls of America. If employer and employee cooperate, I believe that within five or six years, we could very well restore our great industries.

Think with me, and as you do, remember what Sir Francis Bacon suggested: "Read not to contradict and confute; nor to believe and take for granted; nor to find talk and discourse; but to weigh and consider."[7]

I am a preacher, and a preacher, by definition, is a presenter of truth, one who points to promise *and* hope. I hope to do this, for I see how we can move beyond our problems by way of the promise as we actualize the premise.

[7]*The Home Book of Quotations*, ed. Burton Stevenson (New York: Dodd, Mead & Company, 1967), p. 1672.

38

2
The Models:
Two Industries
With Kingdom Values

As I read the Bible, I realized the cause of the death of our steel industry could be attributed directly to the *violation of certain scriptural principles.*

First I looked at my knowledge of scriptural mandates for operating a successful business. Then I looked at the list of reasons to which experts had attributed the demise of the basic steel industry in the United States. That list indicated that the industry had violated almost every scriptural mandate.

My spiritual odyssey had led me to believe that the church could make a significant difference in the world. Not only could we address the issues of prayer in the schools, abortion, or the teaching of creationism, but we could speak "life" into the economic system as well.

Speaking "life" into this system would mean bringing *kingdom values* into business practices. Two questions emerged:

1. What are the specific kingdom values taught in Scripture which would bring renewal in the economic structure?

2. Where could we find *models* in which this value system would be evident?

Eight Principles of Biblical Business Administration

The list of Kingdom values for business operations is not long. In fact, it seems that the profound things of God usually are simple (not simplistic, but simple). Eight major areas were addressed by the inspired writers of the Scripture concerning business ethics.

1. *The Principle of Pruning:*

The first Biblical premise gave me new hope for the renewal of our industrial base. This principle is the seldom-addressed subject of "pruning." When God spoke to the great king of Babylon, Nebuchadnezzer, He did not cut down his leadership to destroy him but to prune him to rise again. Suddenly, I saw the "pruning of God" in our system. He had permitted a system that violated His laws to come to its knees — not to be destroyed, but to be pruned in order for it to grow into a new productive "tree." (See Chapter 5.)

2. *Long-Term Versus Short-Term Goals:*

God is the first "long-term Planner," and Jesus had much to say about this principle. He talked about examining the cost before beginning a project. Corporate conglomerates have violated this basic law of the Kingdom consistently, exchanging short-term profits for long-term planning. (See Chapter 6.)

3. *The Dignity of the Person:*

Foremost of all the principles is the value of the human being. The Bible speaks eloquently that man was crowned with glory and honor, and given dominion over the works of God's hands. (Ps. 8:5,6.) The steel industry, along with most failing business enterprises, violated this basic scriptural foundation for man's works by "dehumanizing" the work environment. (See Chapter 7.)

4. *Non-absentee Landlords:*

The Bible speaks profoundly concerning the "absentee landlord" problem, giving sound advice that land was intended by God to be the property of those who live on the land and derive their income from the land they own. Absentee corporate landlords have, without concern for local communities, run from labor and environmental pollution problems. They have "greenfielded" their manufacturing facilities by moving to new locations, instead of remaining in place and modernizing their present facilities, called "brownfielding" in the industry. (See Chapter 8.)

5. *The Law of Money — Profits:*

Next, I discovered the Biblical law concerning money. The Bible has more to say about money than it does about Heaven or Hell! The Bible makes "profit" not only acceptable, but makes the producing of profit a spiritual mandate for believers. The modern system of business and industry has violated the Biblical mandate concerning money. (See Chapter 9.)

6. *The Law of Creativity:*

In business, generally speaking, the creative person is called an entrepreneur. Entrepreneurship is best manifested, however, in a person who has "let go and let God," or permitted the indwelling Spirit of God to flow through his thinking processes so that his ideas or creativity even in business are inspired. A restoration of Spirit-led entrepreneurial leadership would enable local entrepreneurs to own and operate production facilities in their own communities and return the land to local ownership. (See Chapter 10.)

7. *Servant Leadership:*

Perhaps most important of the eight is the "Law of Servant Leadership." Jesus told us the role of a true leader is exemplified in the King of the universe wearing a towel and washing his followers' feet. The truly well-run companies that survive most any crisis are those companies that never violate this rule. They are the servants of their customers, employees, and even suppliers. (See Chapter 11.)

8. *Spiritual Renewal:*

Last of all was the linking of spiritual renewal or revival to the success of the business sector. Not only did the Scripture teach that each time Israel repented, economic renewal (blessings) followed immediately, but in our own nation, the emergence of the middle class is considered by many historians to be the direct result of the Charles Finney revival in the nineteenth century.[1] (See Chapter 12.)

[I] **will heal their land** (2 Chron. 7:14) is the direct promise of a loving God to the corporate repentance of His people.

---

[1] Jeremy Rifkin with Ted Howard, *The Emerging Order* (New York: G. P. Putnam's Sons, 1979).

I was amazed at how directly the demise of the steel industry paralleled the violation of Biblical laws of business. I knew the revival of those laws could mean the renewal of our basic industry. Our real enemy was not Japan, nor unions, nor even management, but our own violations of God's immutable principles.

The Models

I began to discover also that there were models in America whose very success was based on adherence to the above laws. Two of those models chosen as illustrations in this book are Gibraltar Steel Company and M. Cardone Industries.

The first model is that of my entrepreneurial friend, Dr. Ken Lipke, whose very business structure was built on his adherence to servant leadership, the value of the human being, a strong belief in local ownership of both land and business, and knowledge that entrepreneurial ideas come from God. In almost every way, his leadership of Gibraltar Steel made him a "living model" of what I desire to say in this book.

The second model is that of another very close personal friend, Michael Cardone, Sr. and his son, Michael Cardone, Jr. of Philadelphia, Pennsylvania.

An idea came from God to the poor son of a coal miner many years ago as he was repairing an automobile part in his basement. Michael Cardone, Sr. is living proof that his whole life is involved in making the people he employs realize their own importance and value. He not only is an example of the *rehumanizing* of the business community but has added the dimension of spiritual renewal to the process.

In addition to voluntary thirty-minute inspirational breaks before the work day starts, employees are required to attend "team meetings." During these brief sessions, the topics might be spiritual nuggets or quality, production, or safety points. These always end with prayer concerns and with prayer, although employees are not required to stay. Usually, however, they do stay for prayer. In addition, the Cardones provide chaplains for the many ethnic groups, and capable clergy make hospital calls to the sick and carry out other pastoral duties. This aspect makes the plant a place of Christian discipleship and care as well as a place of employment.

Cardone is an entrepreneur extraordinaire and local owner of both the facilities and the business that provides employment to the community he has always called home. Utilizing money to modernize those facilities and to reward employees for hard work makes the Cardone father-and-son team an exciting model of reindustrialization.

Similar Trends in Some Other Industries

Fortunately, some other industries also have been able to apply similar principles successfully. They have found it is to the advantage of both the owners and the employees to have a closer relationship and for the owner-operators to serve as "servant-leaders."

The law, the men, and the models: all evidence that business can succeed in America again if godly men will obey God's immutable principles and become servant-models.

3

City of God — A Private Journey

February 1983:

What would I say? In just a few minutes, I would be in the office of one of Buffalo's leading industrialists, Dr. Ken Lipke, and I did not really know why. Deep in my soul, I had sensed that I was to meet him and somehow help with his dream. But I did not have the foggiest idea how — or even if — I could help him. I was not even sure he wanted to see me. This appointment had come about in a strange way.

A Drive on the Father Baker Bridge

A few weeks before the day of my surprise appointment with Lipke, I had been driving over the Father Baker Bridge in Buffalo looking at the rusting steel bones of the abandoned steel mill that had fed my hungry city for so many years. Now they said the blast furnaces would cool, the bustling work yards would become deathly quiet. The mammoth mill lay sullen like an evil sore open to the eyes of the passing parade.

As I looked at the skeletons of rusty steel, a strong and powerful idea leaped into my mind, "Could you speak to these dry bones and make them live again?"

I knew the reference. The question was based on the familiar passage in Ezekiel 37:1-14 when the prophet spoke to the dry bones of a dying nation, and through the power of God, those bones took on flesh. Receiving

45

God's breathing spirit in them, they lived again. That is why the powerful thought welling up in my mind was so staggering. I had never applied that verse to industry. Rather it had only been used as a reference to Israel. Somehow, however, I sensed this was a question I would have to face more and more each passing day.

I pondered the strange question. My city of steel had become a debating ground over the issues of industry and the "reindustrialization of America." Far more meaningful to me than the rhetoric was the real and awful hurt I faced each day as I dealt with the unemployed and the unemployable in my dying city. I wanted to believe those steel bones could live again. I wanted so badly to believe that! But was it reasonable? Was it possible? I did not think so, but the question still haunted me.

The plant had been good to my church, my family, and my city. I loved to watch the smoke billow out of those huge stacks as my city proudly made the steel that would become automobiles, bridges, and buildings. The steel industry had been the backbone not only of Buffalo's economy but of the economy of the nation.

Buffalo had always been one of the most exciting cities in the world to me. My favorite drive was Route 5 which leads over the Father Baker Bridge and runs directly along Lake Erie, the site of the Bethlehem Steel plant. In 1963, I came to pastor a small church in my hometown, and finally, I came to live on the shores of Lake Erie. Every night I watched as the sky lit up a brilliant red as the molten steel was poured.

How It All Began

The year I took the pastorate in Buffalo, the mill pulsed with activity as twenty-two thousand steelworkers operated what was then the world's third largest steel facility, the very backbone and ribs of western New York's industrial power structure.

A few years before that, I had lived as a missionary in Asia. Even there I had a keen interest in the steel industry. In 1959, I had watched television in Manila, The Philippines, when 500,000 steelworkers walked off their jobs in a 116-day strike because of a wage dispute. That year, for the first time, the United States imported more steel than it exported. In the wake of that strike, more than 335,000 layoffs occurred in related industries.

Buyers of American steel vowed never again to be so vulnerable to the vagaries of the United States labor-management confrontations. The settlement of that strike presaged future negotiations that by 1982 would see labor costs (including hourly wages and the cost of benefits) skyrocket to $26 per hour for United States steelworkers, while steelworkers in Britain averaged $8.27 per hour, in Japan $10.18 per hour, in West Germany $11.41 per hour, and in South Korea only $1.72 per hour.

Little did I know as I saw the details of this strike unfold that years later I would be so drastically affected by the outcome of something that took place while I was 10,000 miles away in another country.

After I returned to Buffalo as a pastor, I watched over the years as high taxes, union wages, a deterio-rating physical facility, steel imports, declining productivity — and in some cases, an ailing auto industry — transformed the plant I had grown up with into little more than an industrial skeleton. By the fall of 1982, steel production across the nation dropped to 39.9 percent of its capacity, making the lowest level of mill operations since 1938.

All of this became more of a personal tragedy as I watched church members move to other cities. Then my own family was separated when relatives became among those who had to move. My life and the life of my family was engaged in this struggle for survival in a city that once was ruled by steel production.

The Image of an Army

I was a young boy during World War II, and I grew up with names such as Adolph Hitler, Benito Mussolini, and Joseph Stalin being household words. The mere mention of their names struck a chord of fear in our hearts. I remember listening to President Franklin D. Roosevelt on the radio as he declared war on Japan and announced our official and total involvement in the battle against the evil that was terrorizing the world. Soon the names of young men selected for service in the draft were announced daily over the local radio station. We boys listened intently to hear if our fathers were among those chosen to go to war. It was a time of great uncertainty but also a time of great courage.

The spiritual war of the Church seemed so different and distant from the war we were shown in newspapers and on news clips. I wondered, "What is the army of God?"

Pie in the Sky, but Nothing for Today?

Compounding my confusion were traveling evangelists. I loved these flashy, often fleshy, and always fascinating preachers. They were the closest thing to "theater" I had ever seen. Evangelists presented a powerful delivery of God's Word, and in a way, offered a form of sanctified entertainment. They fascinated me.

In all the sermons, I particularly remember the image of the "gold chair." These preachers claimed that when Jesus finally set up His Kingdom, He would sit in a "gold chair," and we would have "peace on earth." There would be justice. Good would overcome evil. We, the "good people," would rule and reign in the earth with Him. However, they warned, until then — until that future moment when Christ sat in the "gold chair" — there was no hope, no peace, and no justice! *We were promised a future but doomed to the present.*

Wars, exploitation, poverty, unemployment, and societal fragmentation indicated that evil indeed was loose in the world and that we had no choice but to endure. What was confusing was that, almost in contradiction, these evangelists proclaimed that the American government was an institution ordained by God through which He ruled "in justice" over us! We were told to obey the government — that in obeying it, we were obeying God as well. I wondered about this.

How could the entire world be evil, yet a part of it also be God's delegated authority? Should Christians not be doing something now to try to change the evil in the world? Should Christians not be active in rooting out and replacing evil with God's Kingdom principles? Was our only alternative just to endure quietly until the "gold chair" was occupied? And was any world system, small or great, really part of God's Kingdom system?

While pondering these questions, I began to read and study the Bible systematically. In the Gospels, I was confronted with the question the disciples asked Christ immediately before He ascended into Heaven: **Lord, will You at this time restore the kingdom to Israel?** (Acts 1:6 NKJV). Jesus answered them with the promise of the infilling of the Holy Spirit and commanded that they become witnesses to all the earth.

The question asked by the disciples essentially was the same one I was asking. They simply asked how long they had to wait until Jesus set up His "gold chair." But Jesus' answer was for them *not* to wait, *but to work.* He sent them into a real and hurting world to do what they could to bring the Kingdom of God **in earth, as it is in heaven** (Matt. 6:10).

It seemed to me then — and still does — that 2,000 years after the Resurrection, Christians are more interested in the future "gold chair" than in bringing His Kingdom of justice, love, reconciliation, grace, and mercy to our world. Did Jesus not harshly chide the scribes and Pharisees for missing the point of faith?

> **Alas for you, scribes and Pharisees, you utter frauds! For you pay your tithe on mint and dill and cummin, and neglect the things which carry far more weight in the Law — justice, mercy and good faith.**
>
> **These are the things you should have observed — without neglecting the others. You blind leaders, for you filter out a mosquito yet swallow a camel.**
>
> **Matthew 23:23,24 JBP**

That we can *and we must* affect our world became obvious to me. But how? What specifically could I do?

Today, I dare to believe the coming "gold chair" is not really the issue for our present dilemma. Rather, we should concentrate on being models of His justice, mercy, and good faith in the midst of a fallen and unjust system. We must do what we can where we are with the resources we have. How do we begin?

The Servant's Throne

In my continued study of Scripture, I began to ask deeper and more difficult philosophical questions. If we are to preach the **gospel of the kingdom** (Mark 1:14), and if peace on earth is to be established by loyalty to a throne, then that throne is not the "gold chair" of the future but a real throne in our present world.

The servant's throne is best illustrated in John 13. The setting is the Passover, or what is known traditionally to Christians as "The Last Supper." Jesus had taken His disciples to an upper room for the sacred feast. There in that room, He wrapped Himself in a towel, bent to his knees, and began washing the feet of the disciples, including those of His betrayer, Judas.

As He washed their feet, the disciples displayed confusion and indignation. A question already had been raised as to who would sit beside Christ when He claimed His "gold chair." Our Lord's response delineated between the ideals of this world's kingdoms and of His Kingdom. Rulers of earthly kingdoms demand servanthood of their subjects, he pointed out. They remove power from the people, excise taxes, and center authority in themselves through the mailed fist of the military or police forces. Jesus showed the disciples in a living object lesson how His Kingdom would be different.

Christ's Kingdom first of all is a kingdom of the heart. Also, He said, the greatest in His Kingdom is the one who gives service to others. *Leadership and authority in God's Kingdom come from servanthood.* The real leader is the one who gives, who yields to others' needs, who rules in love. Christ explained and graphically demonstrated to His disciples that His Kingdom is *not* one of "gold chairs" and thrones but rather one of the "servant's towel."

The more I studied the life of Christ, particularly the passage in John, the more it seemed as if questions I had been asking all my life really had answers. The army of Christ was *not* like the armies of Patton. The "gold chair" of the future paled in the presence of the Christ on His knees bent over washing the feet of the disciples, wearing only the armor of a servant's towel. The ultimate throne I began to see is not a "gold chair" but a throne of servanthood: "the towel and basin."

If the army of our King is to make an impact, the promised-future-but-doomed-present attitude of the Church during this century must be discarded. Rather, there must arise a people willing to overcome the world — not by force but by servanthood. We must become a society of servants, seeking the good of others. We must become a nation of leaders who rule from our knees.

My life had been clouded by a lifetime of bad philosophy. Now the Kingdom of God was coming into a clear perspective. The Church must have real impact on the world *now*, not in the sweet by and by. If I could first learn to live as a servant, then perhaps I could influence servanthood in my church, community, industry, government, and all society — society that too often abdicated the servant's role for a throne of greed.

Could it be that our business system has failed because Christians have been poor witnesses of Christ's intention for them? Have we too long seen this world system as evil? Are all things made and created for Him to rule over and through? If this is true, then God's people can penetrate with a servant principle and make the system productive and profitable.

My Personal Dissatisfaction

Life is an ever-learning experience, and these new ideas of servant leadership gripped me. I had known a measure of success. I often lectured on the subject of success at pastors' conferences, business meetings, and from my own pulpit. I had enjoyed a "successful" evangelistic ministry, and for twenty years, I had been the pastor of a single church. During that time, the church grew to become the largest evangelical assembly in the northeastern United States. With five branch churches each Sunday, we had about 7,000 worshippers. But I felt there was a growing need for further involvement in an area outside the church world.

Something in my heart burned deeply. It was a quiet, yet persistent sense of dissatisfaction in "merely" pastoring a large church. Oddly, some years earlier, another sense of dissatisfaction over lack of church growth had led me to a deep spiritual renewal that was followed by a virtual explosion of growth in our church. In fact, I wrote of that experience in a book entitled *The Exploding Church*, published in 1979.

Often I felt like a spectator as God built up the church, first in my heart and then as a physical reality. What was happening seemed a repeat of this earlier work but on a much broader basis. My heart was marked by a growing and haunting sense of dissatisfaction so marked that I wondered if I were to leave the ministry.

What was the point of simply getting people into church to fill pews and membership rolls? What was the point of helping them overcome sinful lifestyles, yet not effecting positive changes in their real worlds? Truly, I thought, if the Church is to be real, it must be able to affect the world in which it exists.

Although I remained a strong historic premillennialist and believed in the imminent Rapture of the Church, I was becoming disturbed by the apparent fatalism toward our world that seemed to be the result of my own emphasis on that impending Rapture. That fatalism seemed to result in a lack of concern for God-ordained sociological responsibilities of all Christians. Since then, I have come to understand that a premillennialist eschatological view need not result in a fatalistic view of the world. By its very character, premillennialism mandates sociological responsibility through its emphasis on the presence of evil in society.

Premillennialism constantly reaffirms the teaching of Jesus as he talked about "wheat and tares" growing together, and his constant warning to the disciples that

His Kingdom would create "conflict" and not immediate peace. He further chided them for their mistaken conclusion that their presence on "gold chairs" in Jerusalem would eliminate evil from the earth. This very presence of evil as taught by Christ is truly the cornerstone of premillennial philosophy.

Premillennialism also can well affirm our relationship to the evil in the world and our participation in the accompanying conflict. The role of salt, light, and leaven is in reality a hallmark of our premillennial view of the very presence of evil, and our responsibility to *be* that salt, light, and leaven. We also agree that Jesus' constant reminder of "persecution" to come against His disciples was an indication that He knew they would be involved in this conflict with evil. The obvious conclusion is that the presence of evil in our society mandates an accompanying impact we have to make in order to be the prophesied "overcomers" (Rev. 21:7) in the midst of the conflict.

As I personally wrestled with this particular world view and broadened my own understanding of my personal premillennial position, I began to see the Church as more than a monastic institution called to prepare people for death or an impending Rapture. I began to see the Church as an army mandated to occupy until Jesus returned, an agency called to infiltrate the sociological problems of the world created by the continuing presence of evil Jesus prophesied would exist until His return. In fact, this world view of mandated social involvement gave me a stronger basis for my premillennial position.

I also noted that the Rapture itself took on new meaning, as I saw the very purpose of "going up" to meet Him was to "come again" with Him, so that we would be involved directly in the final conflict at Megiddo. My own eschatological position enhanced, I realigned my preaching to a point where no longer did I point people to the "other world" but preached that we are to be witnesses to *this* world in every sphere of life.

The Eternal Thrust

As I pondered, I thought about the announcement Jesus had made, **the kingdom of heaven is at hand** (Matt. 4:17). This Kingdom was to be salt, light, and leaven that would fill all the earth. But fill all the earth with *what*? As I preached Kingdom principles, this *what* became more of an issue for me.

We must affect our world, I reasoned, and become light, salt, and leaven in our society. We must project God's Kingdom principles into the fabric of our fractured world. Jesus insisted, **Occupy til I come** (Luke 19:13). We were to work not just wait. I began to see that *to occupy* meant "to become profitable, to expand His Kingdom, to take back ground from Satan, to reclaim God's world and God's system, and to redeem His earth through servant leadership."

It was during the days when I was pondering all this that God brought Dr. Ken Lipke into my life. Driving to his office that day, I wondered what I would say — but even more, I wondered where God was leading me to put into practice what I had been learning.

In another steel city, Pittsburgh, frustrated unemployed workers carried their cry into the churches. They felt the Church had coddled the rich for too long and ignored the plight of the poor. Some workers systematically and insistently interrupted worship services, demanding not only to be heard but demanding action from the churches. One minister's sympathy led him into confrontations and outspoken sermons that resulted in his being jailed, as well as barred from his pulpit and his parish. The Pittsburgh problem became more confrontational and violent. Some of the unemployed refused to wait quietly or be placated with promises.

But in Buffalo, people waited in hopelessness without the energy or will to protest. I do not condone violent or hostile confrontations. However, I can identify with the frustrations and helplessness of the unemployed. Too often the Church *has* held apart from the turmoil, instead of speaking to questions raised. Now God was moving me and my congregation to help in constructive and meaningful ways.

The Church Has Incredible Power

I had come to believe the Church has incredible power available to it, power to put into practice the principles of Christ and to make a real difference in the world system. That day, as I drove to meet Lipke, I felt my prayers had been heard. I was being thrust into a whole new world. The words rang in my spirit, *Speak to the dry bones, 'Rise and walk.'* (Ezek. 37:4.) But how could I *speak*, and what did "speaking" mean?

I was beginning a spiritual odyssey that could enable me to play a role in a very real drama of our modern world. I was on my way to meet a man attempting to "speak life" into a dying steel plant through entrepreneurial giftedness. As I watched this exciting drama from the front lines, I was to discover God's laws for renewal of the economic sector and to meet men who believed in and obeyed those laws. These men are living proof that, if we return to Biblical laws of business practice, basic industry can live again.

This book is my way of "speaking life" back into any dying business in God's world, even the industrial system of America.

4

The Impossible Dream

My appointment with a man who believed an "impossible dream" came about in an unusual way.

One day, as I watched a newscast on local television, the face of a leading industrialist flashed across the screen. I was shocked to hear Dr. Ken Lipke say he wanted to purchase the Bethlehem Steel plant and bring it back to life.

The next morning, I received a call from one of my parishioners who said he wanted me to meet Dr. Lipke. I knew getting an appointment with him would be almost impossible. He was busy talking with mayors, congressmen, governors, and leaders of industry. Why would he ever want to talk with a preacher? But my friend said he was Dr. Lipke's friend and would call for an appointment.

Saturdays are my sermon study days, so I was in my office that Saturday ignoring the phone. After several hours of study, I looked at the phone as the line lit up. I do not know why I looked at it just at that moment and even less why I picked up the phone.

A man's voice said, "Dr. Lipke has a whole stack of phone messages, but it seems yours is always on top of the stack. What can he do for you?"

I hesitated, not knowing what to say.

Then I blurted out, "I would like to see him."

However, I knew as soon as I said it that even if I were able to get an appointment, it probably would be weeks before Dr. Lipke had any time open to see me.

To my surprise, the man said, "Fine. Come over right now."

Still almost in shock at getting an immediate appointment — and on a Saturday, at that — I headed toward the industrialist's plush office, pondering all the way. What would I say, and in the first place, what did I want? I did not really know, but I was soon to find out. That meeting led me to a determined dedication to speak the words of life to industry and labor. Dr. Lipke has helped me see that the dead bones of industry *can* live again.

I walked into Dr. Lipke's office on that fateful Saturday unaware that I was meeting a man destined to become a close friend. I knew a few facts about him, but I did not know that he had a stubborn vision for steelmaking in western New York to be something more than a forlorn memory.

I knew that prior to 1972, he had been a chiropractor. Then he moved into business consulting and very shortly afterwards became a steel executive. Now his plant, Gibraltar Steel, was pulsing with life and growing. It was one of the very few steel companies that had survived the recession and actually earned a profit.

He looked up from his desk and said, "Why are you here?"

I told him that honestly, I did not know, but that I felt divinely directed to see him. At that time, I knew nothing of his religious beliefs or background. I told him of my belief in his "dream" and of my desire as a clergyman to support him.

Soon the conversation turned into an intense dialogue between two people who believed in one another. When I told him about "divine direction," he told me of the emotional upheaval of the past few days in his own life.

Imprint From Childhood

He said, "It was 3 a.m., and I tossed and turned on my bed, unable to sleep. This was not unusual. However, as I lay awake, I began to think about the closing of Bethlehem Steel. It greatly disturbed me, because the factory had been an unshakable institution in our city for so long.

"I thought of my dad and remembered when he lost his job in a similar circumstance. I was just a boy at the time, but I still remembered how the light in his eyes had gone out. His world was fragile suddenly, and he was more frightened than he had ever believed possible. Security, once taken for granted, was an elusive concept now. Dad worried over how he was going to provide food and other necessities for his family.

"I knew that now the light had gone from the eyes of the unemployed in Buffalo. They knew what was happening — but did not know what to do. They were in many ways helpless. The steel plant would close, and there would be no other jobs for most of them. What jobs that could be found would not come close to providing the income they had been earning.

"That night as I lay sleepless, the dream of bringing the steel mill back to life was born.

"During this time of upheaval at the steel mill, my father — now much older — had a heart attack and was taken to the hospital. I was afraid I was going to lose this man I loved and admired so much. When I visited him in the hospital, I told him of my dream.

"He said, 'Ken, you save the plant for me, and I'll do my best to stay alive for you.'

"I knew then that I would risk everything necessary to realize this dream of saving a dying steel plant."

As a result of his determination, Dr. Lipke chose an already arranged speaking engagement at a local garden club the next day to make his announcement to the public. He would resign as chairman of Gibraltar Steel and attempt to purchase and revitalize the Bethlehem Steel facility.

With the media in attendance, his announcement was made — the newscast that I had seen, and which had initiated our meeting and subsequent friendship. Instead of the hope he had intended, his announcement brought skepticism and even hostility! However, the die was cast.

He said, "I am at the start of what apparently has become the most controversial odyssey of my life. At every juncture I am encountering excruciatingly difficult, and so far even insurmountable, problems. The situation has proven more serious and complex than I first realized. But, still, I'm determined to continue seeking solutions."

I ended the conversation by inviting him to come to our church and publicly explain his dream and the intended purchase of the Bethlehem facility.

In March 1983, Dr. Lipke stepped into the pulpit of the Tabernacle, and in both services, told of his "impossible dream." Some believed, and some did not. But we were about to witness events over the next few months that would almost result in the salvation of a major steel mill.

He became a blurred kaleidoscope of perpetual motion. Among other things, he sought potential investors, "jaw-boned" labor to accept a lower hourly wage, sought financial concessions from state government, spoke at scores of public meetings to gain support for his takeover plan. Above all else, he attempted to convince Bethlehem Steel to sell the Lackawanna facility to him as part of a long-range plan in which he would sell cheaper-produced steel back to them.

Dr. Lipke had to establish his own credibility with Bethlehem and convince them to have confidence in the marketplace. As he marched into the forbidding swamps of the Bethlehem situation, there was a more subtle obstacle to overcome: the attitude of the business community.

Banks Turn Deaf Ears

In many ways, the Buffalo area business community was as class-ridden as Edwardian England. The banking establishment, very conservative and "old money," viewed with suspicion and envy the "new breed" of self-made millionaires like Dr. Lipke, whose "tall-in-the-saddle" promotional devices only irritate the traditional lending institutions.

On more than one occasion Dr. Lipke, sitting across a desk from a reluctant bank official, peered at the banker and thought, "Aren't you chilly sitting there in nothing but your pinched pessimism?"

Twelve years earlier, some of the same banks, taking full cognizance of his background as a chiropractor, had turned a deaf ear when he was putting together a group of investors to purchase Gibraltar Steel, an 18-year-old manufacturer of steel strapping and cold-rolled strip steel at the time.

As the weeks passed into late winter and on into the early spring, Dr. Lipke was frustrated by an array of factors, not the least of which was a confidentiality agreement in which he had agreed not to disclose details of his negotiations. This created the credibility gap. Media queries had to be greeted with amiable vagueness. He also fell victim to a cavalcade of events which threw off his timing:

— Two days after his announcement, Congressman Jack Kemp told Dr. Lipke to put his plan on the back burner until labor and government exhausted efforts to get Bethlehem to reverse its decision to shut down.

— Bethlehem rejected a union proposal that would have cut labor costs in exchange for keeping the plant in operation.

— An official of the United Steelworkers blasted Dr. Lipke for suggesting that labor accept a $15-per-hour package in a Lipke-run plant.

For weeks, Dr. Lipke tugged at the sleeves of state government to secure help. Not much happened. Finally, he took the advice of friends and confronted New York Governor Mario Cuomo during a live television show in Buffalo.

During a question and answer period, the steel executive rose from a front-row seat and told the startled governor that he had received minimum help from the state.

Dr. Lipke declared, "I am the one possible ray of hope for this community to save steelmaking."

After a brief but spirited exchange, Governor Cuomo advised Dr. Lipke to explain his plan to the state commerce commissioner "so we can deal with the facts and not just empty aspirations." An hour later, someone from the commerce department called Dr. Lipke and asked if he could meet with Commissioner William Donohue in two days.

The meeting, held at Gibraltar Steel, began in a very chilly atmosphere May 27, 1983, because Mr. Donohue and his staff thought he had been coerced into the meeting by the public exchange between Dr. Lipke and the governor. The 4 p.m. meeting promised to have all the gaity of a tax audit. Mr. Donohue and Dr. Lipke were joined by Brian Lipke, who had succeeded his father as Gibraltar chairman, and Richard O'Brien, Gibraltar vice president.

State Holds Out Only Straws

Dr. Lipke discussed his takeover plan with Mr. Donohue at a level of detail heretofore only known to Bethlehem Steel officials. In spite of Donohue's skepticism, the meeting ended on a friendly note. A couple of weeks later, in fact, Mr. Donohue said publicly that on the basis of their meeting, he was encouraged about preserving some of the operations at the Lackawanna plant. He said his view of the takeover had changed "180 degrees" on the basis of his close perusal of the details involved.

However, on June 14, Dr. Lipke announced that he was abandoning his plan for a takeover of the entire plant in favor of a partial takeover. One factor in his decision may have been touched on by Lawrence Reger, chairman of Western New York's Mader Capital Inc., who had pledged $5 million to the campaign and had helped Dr. Lipke in his purchase of Gibraltar years earlier. Mr. Reger openly wondered if Bethlehem would be willing to help a potential competitor buy the Lackawanna plant.

Throughout all of these events, however, Dr. Lipke and Bethlehem's President Walter Williams remained friends.

October 14, 1983, Bethlehem workers ran the last massive steel ingot through several finishing operations. The heating ovens, conveyor lines, and control panels were then shut down.

An era had ended.

Meanwhile, Dr. Lipke was reviewing his four-month odyssey, a classic engagement of ambitions, actions, and events; and I had come to a growing conviction that "the good news is that the bad news is wrong." I knew that we could, and we must, solve industry's problems.

During the Seventies, more than thirty million jobs had been lost as a direct result of closing steel plants. Another two million jobs were lost because of plants that were "relocated." When all factors were tabulated, more than thirty-eight million people had been put out of jobs. What caused such a sharp reversal in ten years? The cause was some very fundamental things that are still happening and will have a profound and continuing effect on American business and industry in general, and on the steel industry in particular. Two primary causes are a focus on domestic concerns and an increased access by foreign industry to United States markets.

A Focus on Domestic Concerns

This emphasis began to characterize much of American life shortly after the ending of the Vietnam War. Throughout its relatively brief history, the United States has been involved in world events of great magnitude, with subsequent rebuilding and development necessitated by each horrendous event.

The Marshall Plan in Europe and MacArthur's redevelopment efforts in Japan following World War II are prime examples of the strength and bountiful resources of the American economy, not to mention the colossal effort required for the war itself.

However, these ventures into the world economic arena have sharply diminished in recent years. Perhaps many Americans have become tired of carrying the world's burden on their shoulders and now prefer to concentrate on the challenges still confronting us on the domestic scene. Unemployment, poverty, environmental pollution, inflation, and high taxation are at the top of America's internal concerns.

Historically, it has been easy when a feeling of global weariness sets in for Americans to make a temporary retreat within our own borders and partially shut out the cares of the world. Our geographical location has allowed us at will to ignore many concerns troubling other parts of the world. Also, we have always had a comfortable supply of essential raw materials as well as a vast domestic market.

Other nations of the world often have fewer options of involvement. Japan has traditionally had a strong international awareness and involvement because of necessity. Japanese people are inveterate world travelers, faithfully gathering the "better ideas" essential to maintain high levels of productivity. This, in turn, guarantees continued penetration of world markets.

Our isolation has been beneficial at times, but it also is a burden. As we approach the last decade of the 20th century, we see the United States has not achieved a strong international awareness even yet. We have been slow to recognize and respond to the competitive challenges springing forth from many corners of the world.

Increased Foreign Access

The increased access of foreign industry to domestic markets seems to have caught most people by surprise, when actually, it has been going on for some time. We laughed when the first Volkswagen "Beetles" were introduced, not realizing that "Beetles" would become "Rabbits," and breed furiously. This was the method by which foreign steel entered the United States marketplace.

Since then, many other foreign car manufacturers have copied Volkswagen's lead. And it did not stop with vehicles. Today, we import motorcycles, cameras, televisions, all types of electronic equipment, and myriads of other items.

This strong penetration of foreign goods was encouraged by many factors: the United States market is vast and affluent and makes an attractive target, and the United States market is usually first to seek innovative products of all types and in all price ranges. We are a viable market for new products. All of this is not necessarily bad, but it often creates more problems than it solves. Other nations seem to have a greater ability to handle the problem of foreign trade.

In the case of steel, some specifics involved were that United States firms stuck to old-fashioned open hearth blast furnaces, while foreign steel firms turned toward oxygen furnaces, several times more efficient and productive. There also was the problem of high wages. The steelworkers' pay of $26 per hour was so far out of line with the rest of the world that American steel could no longer successfully compete on the international market or even against imported steel on the domestic market.

In spite of slogans and anger, the problem will not go away. And we must deal with it.

Principle Number One:
God's Pruning Season

5

The Pruning of America's Business and Industry

Through the years, I have watched with fascination the pruning of trees and shrubbery. While the initial cutting back seemed ugly, the pruning process was necessary for further fruitfulness. Fruit trees left unpruned and uncared for will not only produce less fruit, but what is produced will be smaller. Eventually, the tree will produce nothing at all, becoming useless. The Bible speaks explicitly about pruning for production. One of the earliest examples is in the prophetic book of Daniel.

King Nebuchadnezzar had a dream he did not understand. Relating it to seer Daniel for interpretation, the Babylonian potentate said:

> "I saw a very tall tree out in a field, growing higher and higher into the sky until it could be seen by everyone in all the world. Its leaves were fresh and green, and its branches were weighted down with fruit, enough for everyone to eat. Wild animals rested beneath its shade and birds sheltered in its branches, and all the world was fed from it. Then as I lay there dreaming, I saw one of God's angels coming down from heaven.

> "He shouted, 'Cut down the tree; lop off its branches; shake off its leaves, and scatter its fruit. Get the animals out from under it and the birds from its branches, but leave its stump and roots in the ground, banded with a chain of iron and brass, surrounded

by the tender grass. Let the dews of heaven drench him and let him eat grass with the wild animals! For seven years let him have the mind of an animal instead of a man. For this has been decreed by the Watchers, demanded by the Holy Ones. The purpose of this decree is that all the world may understand that the Most High dominates the kingdoms of the world, and gives them to anyone he wants to, even the lowliest of men!' "

The holy record concludes the fascinating story:

"O Belteshazzar, that was my dream; now tell me what it means. For no one else can help me; all the wisest men of my kingdom have failed me. But you can tell me, for the spirit of the holy gods is in you."

Then Daniel sat there stunned and silent for an hour, aghast at the meaning of the dream. Finally the king said to him: "Belteshazzar, don't be afraid to tell me what it means."

Daniel replied: "Oh, that the events foreshadowed in this dream would happen to your enemies, my lord, and not to you! For the tree you saw growing so tall, reaching high into the heavens for all the world to see, with its fresh green leaves, loaded with fruit for all to eat, the wild animals living in its shade, with its branches full of birds — that tree, Your Majesty, is you. For you have grown strong and great; your greatness reaches up to heaven, and your rule to the ends of the earth.

"Then you saw God's angel coming down from heaven and saying, 'Cut down the tree and destroy it, but leave the stump and the roots in the earth surrounded by tender grass, banded with a chain of iron and brass. Let him be wet with the dew of heaven. For seven years let him eat grass with the animals of the field.'

"Your Majesty, the Most High God has decreed
— and it will surely happen — that your people will
chase you from your palace, and you will live in the
fields like an animal, eating grass like a cow, your
back wet with dew from heaven. For seven years this
will be your life, until you learn that the Most High
God dominates the kingdoms of men, and gives power
to anyone he chooses. But the stump and the roots
were left in the ground! This means that you will get
your kingdom back again, when you have learned that
heaven rules.

"O King Nebuchadnezzar, listen to me — stop
sinning; do what you know is right; be merciful to
the poor. Perhaps even yet God will spare you.' "

Daniel 4:10-27 TLB

Note carefully that the purpose of pruning is
outlined by the Bible:

"The purpose of this decree is that all the world
may understand that the Most High dominates the
kingdoms of the world, and gives them to anyone he
wants to, even the lowliest of men!"

Daniel 4:17 TLB

A Heart of Pride

When arrogance reigns, the common person
suffers. Therefore, a caring God strikes at the heart of
pride and brings nations, industries, and people back
to His intended purpose for them. Sadly,
Nebuchadnezzar ignored Daniel!

But all these things happened to Nebuchadnezzar.
Twelve months after this dream, he was strolling on
the roof of the royal palace in Babylon, and saying,
"I, by my own mighty power, have built this beautiful

75

city as my royal residence, and as the capital of my empire."

While he was still speaking these words, a voice called down from heaven, "O King Nebuchadnezzar, this message is for you: You are no longer ruler of this kingdom. You will be forced out of the palace to live with the animals in the fields, and to eat grass like the cows for seven years until you finally realize that God parcels out the kingdoms of men and gives them to anyone he chooses."

That very same hour this prophecy was fulfilled. Nebuchadnezzar was chased from his palace and ate grass like the cows, and his body was wet with dew; his hair grew as long as eagles' feathers, and his nails were like birds' claws.

Daniel 4:28-33 TLB

One thing becomes crystal clear in this incident from Old Testament history — and through practical life experiences: Pain often brings change. And the greater the pain, the more dramatic the change. Look at what happened at the end of Nebuchadnezzar's seven years:

"At the end of seven years I, Nebuchadnezzar, looked up to heaven, and my sanity returned, and I praised and worshiped the Most High God and honored him who lives forever, whose rule is everlasting, his kingdom evermore. All the people of the earth are nothing when compared to him; he does whatever he thinks best among the hosts of heaven, as well as here among the inhabitants of earth. No one can stop him or challenge him, saying, 'What do you mean by doing these things?' When my mind returned to me, so did my honor and glory and kingdom. My counselors and officers came back to me and I was reestablished as head of my kingdom, with even greater honor than before.

"Now, I, Nebuchadnezzar, praise and glorify and honor the King of Heaven, the Judge of all, whose every act is right and good; for he is able to take those who walk proudly and push them into the dust!"

Daniel 4:34-37 TLB

Pruning and pain in the Babylonian king's life produced reverence, renewal, and restoration. He fulfilled the words of the pragmatic preacher:

See the way God does things and fall into line. Don't fight the facts of nature. Enjoy prosperity whenever you can, and when hard times strike, realize that God gives one as well as the other — so that everyone will realize that nothing is certain in this life.

Ecclesiastes 7:13,14 TLB

I deeply believe that what is happening in the steel industry is a pruning process. I believe we need not give up to the inundation of foreign steel or lack of modernization. *We can and must compete.* However, we need to realize that other parts of the American business and industrial system may come under the pruning process as well.

Our system is in need of pruning in order for new life to grow. In many places, our system has deteriorated badly. Business and industry have become fragmented, marked by hostility and suspicion. Management and unions often are mortal enemies. They are warring camps who see each other at cross purposes. Government is perceived as an enemy of industry. But there is a bright note. Even after pruning takes place, the stumps and roots still are there, and new growth is made possible.

Human nature tends to be anarchist and perfectionist when confronting a system needing change. We wrongly assume everything must be destroyed in the old system, and something entirely new must take its place — like the legend of the Phoenix bird.

The roots of labor unions can remain. The roots of industrial conglomerates can remain. The roots of government guidelines can remain. But, as the system is pruned, evil abuses must be cut away so the tree of American business and industry can grow fruitful.

We must remember it is "the evil one" who wishes death and destruction. Satan's goal is total destruction and chaos through fragmentation and corruption. God's goal is restoration and redemption through pruning.

Nebuchadnezzar learned that unless he was connected to the creativity of God, he was no more than an animal acting on instinct. Joined to the flow of God's creativity, however, he was able to build an empire. Truly, he was a king only when he allowed God's image within him to be properly actualized by the Holy Spirit.

God's Dominion Is Everlasting

By the end of the story, we see that Nebuchadnezzar came to a profound realization that God's dominion is everlasting, and all on earth are as nothing without Him. He saw a God Who can and will do anything according to His will, even if men deny His existence. Nebuchadnezzar also saw his sanity, position, and wealth returned to him through the grace of God. He had been pruned, but not destroyed. New growth could take place, resulting in the return to the productivity evident prior to the pruning. The king finally knew Who was truly King.

God rules the earth through people. He gave us dominion over the earth and wishes to rule through us. He only asks that we recognize His sovereignty over us. He is King, and we are kings, born to rule as He rules through us.

As Nebuchadnezzar learned the profound truth that the "old" system needed pruning, he learned also that God's intention is to bring life back to the tree.

Restoration is a Biblical concept that runs throughout the Scripture.

The Biblical premise of "restoration" through the process of *pruning* is being violated by American industry. We have assumed wrongly that smokestack industries must either be replaced or relocated to other cities to survive. The words used in industrial America are *disinvestment* and *greenfielding*.

Instead of reinvesting in present facilities (a process known as *brownfielding*) and making those facilities live again to serve the communities that have given them millions in profit over a period of many decades, giant corporations have decided to *greenfield* or rebuild their plants in other cities. Our government has even contributed to this problem by offering tax advantages that make moving more profitable for the corporations than remaining and rebuilding.

Disinvestment has seemingly become more profitable for the massive corporations than *reinvestment* in their present properties. It is my feeling that our system of business and industry is in actuality violating a scriptural mandate to "dig around the tree and refertilize."

Greenfielding is the accepted form of running from the difficulty of labor problems, ecological problems, or difficult local or state governmental problems. It has been seemingly profitable to have a major multinational corporation move its plant from the northeast rustbelt to the sunbelt, or even to the borders of Mexico, in order to obtain cheaper labor, more liberal ecological restraints, or cheaper taxation. Little concern is given to the huge and productive labor force left behind or the devastation present in the community.

I submit that — although disinvestment and greenfielding seemingly were, in the short term, economically profitable — in the long term, the de-emphasis on the value of the human being that was demonstrated by these practices has nearly destroyed basic industry in the United States.

The opposite is true in Japan where the emphasis on the value of the human being has resulted in reinvestment in physical facilities, and in the long term, on the profitability and viability of the whole system of basic manufacturing.

Restoration Through Local Ownership

Perhaps the major enemy of *greenfielding* is local ownership of a manufacturing facility. An entrepreneur who has grown up and lived an entire life in one community would hardly choose to *greenfield* his factory to a community in another state or country in order to earn additional short-term profits.

The Bible speaks much about the benefits of local ownership. In the law of Moses, God established the "Year of Jubilee" under which all property was to be returned to its original owner. Even though a family would get into severe financial difficulty and borrow against a piece of real estate, at the end of fifty years, that property would be returned to the family.

Therefore, it is obvious from Scripture that land would continue to be owned by resident landlords rather than by absentee landlords in a distant city or country. Certainly, if this were done, there would be no reason to *greenfield* to another city.

Another interesting concept in the Bible is in the book of Daniel where God showed the prophet that the kingdom would be taken from Babylon and given to the Medes and Persians. Then the Medes and Persians later returned the land of Judah to its "resident owners," those Jewish people who chose to return from exile in Babylon to their own land when permitted to do so.

Also, the Bible shows that when the Israelites first moved into the land of Canaan, the Promised Land, that God divided the land between the twelve tribes, with each having a certain region or area on which to live.

Is it possible that there is a "pattern" in the Bible for us to follow in these matters? Is it even possible there is a *mandate* from God for the residents of a community to own the industries located there?

Driving through my own city, I saw the devastation that moving the grain industry and the steel industry caused in Buffalo. Absentee landlords have left thousands of acres of valuable real estate littered with decaying grain silos that would cost millions to move and rusting blast furnaces on valuable waterfront property where the cost of removal or restoration would exceed the value of the ground.

Is this perhaps a spiritual problem? A violation of Biblical law? Perhaps it is time for America to celebrate a "Year of Jubilee."

Models Exemplify the Way

Both of our *models* are examples of strong local ownership. Gibraltar is owned by a man who is an "evangelist" for his community. Riding in his boat or helicopter, he constantly extols the beauty and virtues of his community. Dr. Lipke lives and works in Buffalo, not because it is convenient, nor even because it is more profitable, but because he loves his home and feels a responsibility to it. Many other cities and states have made attractive offers that would make life easier and more profitable.

The same is true of the second *model*, M. Cardone Industries.

I met Michael Cardone, Sr. for the first time in 1955, when he was a young man starting out in business. Already successful, he loved his city — Philadelphia. With gusto, he would take me to the famed Bookbinders Restaurant and extol the virtues of that famous place. We drove through the streets of South Philadelphia where every cobblestone was special to this man of many talents. He does business in Philadelphia not because it is convenient but because he is a "resident landlord" living in and for his community.

When the ethnic mix changed, he adapted his philosophy of business, integrating these new ethnic groups into his staff and expanding his factory in order to employ more of the new people. These are *his* people, because they live in *his* city.

A Better Alternative

We must not accept the alleged truth that we are to become an information society. When major authors and economists say this nation has become the information capital of the world, and therefore, we need to let other nations manufacture the steel, build the ships, the automobiles, or the appliances we use in our homes, I submit that this thinking needs to be re-examined. The pruning of our system was not for devastation, but rather for the regrowing of a truly healthy industrial base.

I believe a combination of a healthy "third wave" information society, linked with a strong industrial base to utilize that information is a better alternative.

If this is not done, we will face a crisis of national security. A nation that cannot make its own steel, automobiles, airplanes, tanks, or guns is a nation that is defenseless. As we were oil dependent in 1973 to the Arab nations, we now have become "steel dependent" on other nations. Allied nations many times become enemy nations from one generation to the next.

A question must be asked, "Are we dependent on our enemies for the weapons of a future war?"

Something must be done to save basic industry in America.

Principle Number Two:
Long-Term Versus Short-Term Goals

6

Faith: Where "the Rubber Meets the Road"

Jewish proselyte Walter Kaufmann reviewed the religions of the world in his book, *Religions in Four Dimensions*, and commented:

> Religion is not merely or even mainly a matter of what people say or write in books but also of what they do in following their religion, or of what their religion does to them.[1]

Kaufmann also asserted:

> Intellectually, most philosophy of religion is sterile. Morally, it often seems to be a pastime that diverts some academics from hearing the voice of their brothers' blood.[2]

While some might disagree with Kaufmann's conclusions, they do serve to remind us that faith must be "where the rubber meets the road."

At times, we are tempted to feel our efforts to "Christianize" labor and management are futile. We look at our wounded world and wonder if there is a

---

[1]Walter Kaufmann, *Religion in Four Dimensions* (New York: Reader's Digest Press, 1976), p. 19.

[2]Ibid., p. 20.

loving God who really cares. Perhaps we can identify with many Jews. Kaufmann says of them:

> Many Jews do not see how they could possibly believe in God any more, after Auschwitz. Nor does Auschwitz stand alone. Other camps come to mind, and not only millions of murdered Jews but also slaughters in India and Pakistan — for the sake of religion — and in Biafra, Vietnam, and Bangladesh, as well as the fate of millions of black people who are starving to death in Africa.[3]

Circumstances must not determine faith. Just as in the dead of night, the light seems impossible and far away, so the evils of man have blotted out the sun for some. Lacking understanding of God's way, will, and Word, people in trouble sometimes are quick to throw Him overboard or claim He is dead or at least senile. What they fail to realize is that the morning will come. And even now in the darkness of our night, there are millions still holding up the light in their homes and on their jobs.

Show Forth the Light of God

We have been recruited by God to move into the marketplace to show forth His light. Even though some are so blinded by rage and hate that they cannot see the light, it should still be there. Others, loving the darkness, will seek to put out the light. Thus our task is never easy, and our faith is always on the line. But this is the hour God has called us to His work. May we rise to the challenge and live by His light rather than the darkness of our day.

---

[3]Ibid., p. 107.

Dr. Robert Schuller recently said on a television program, "There is nothing more dangerous than religion in the hands of a negative person."

History many times bears this out, as "religious" persons have used their own Pharisaical demand for the rightness of their views to hurt or even kill others. Although the Nazi regime's policy that resulted in the death of millions of Jews was based on race, not religion, religious prejudice is blamed by many scholars for keeping the average German citizen from protesting racial persecution.

German philosopher Friedrich Wilhelm Nietzsche said, "The earth has a skin and that skin has diseases; one of its diseases is called man."[4]

This negative and un-Biblical view not only contributed to the Nazi reign of terror but easily could produce many other similar tragedies unless the Church seriously reexamines her role in society. Perhaps it would be well to remember that even in the darkness of the Nazi night, God sent deeply devoted men and women to hold up the light. When it seemed bloodthirsty dictators greedily gobbled up Nietzsche's dogma and turned on their fellowmen with rapacious fury, there were flickering rays of hope.

Nietzsche cursed the darkness of the world with his philosophy, but other people became "lighted candles" in the Nazi darkness.

---

[4]*Portable Curmudgeon*, ed. John Winokur (New York: New American Library, 1987), p. 189.

One of these "rays of hope" was Dietrich Bonhoeffer, who was born six years after Nietzsche died. This other German totally rejected the morality inherent in Nietzsche's philosophy. A creative, courageous German pastor and professor, he was killed by the Nazis a few days before the Allied victory in 1945.

After years of authoring books hailed for their original scholarship and after doing graduate work at Union Seminary in New York, he joined the faculty of the University of Berlin, teaching there until expelled by the Nazis in 1936 for denouncing the Fuhrer cult as "idolatry."

In 1935, he took over the direction of a by-then illegal church training college for young German pastors. Then he wrote *The Cost of Discipleship*[5] in 1937, an account of his personal experiences. He castigated the easy, culture-religion then masquerading as the Gospel in Germany. Through American friends who engineered his escape, he could have remained in safety from 1939 until the war was over. However, understanding that being a Christian means taking risks, he returned to his homeland where he took many risks by passing on details of the German resistance movement to British intelligence. He also met with the ringleaders of an unsuccessful attempt to assassinate Hitler.

Arrested in 1943, he spent the time until his death in early 1945 ministering to fellow inmates and guards alike. During this time, he smuggled scraps of writings

---

[5]Reprinted with permission of Macmillan Publishing Company from *The Cost of Discipleship* by Dietrich Bonhoeffer. Copyright © 1959 by SCM Press, Ltd.

out to friends, scraps published and widely read after the war.[6]

Bonhoeffer insisted that a person called by God is obligated to make use of his freedom with a sense of responsibility to conserve the divine ordering of life. A Christian, he maintained, must be willing to act, suffer, and if necessary, to die.

He maintained that a Christian is a simple person living in the midst of perplexities, questions, and tasks who throws himself on the mercy of God and takes the risks of living responsibly." He said a Christian is not a religious person or someone trying to be saintly.[7]

The 39-year-old pastor who had warned against "cheap grace"[8] followed his own beliefs that when a man is called by Jesus, he is called to come and die if necessary. He was hanged April 9, 1945, by Hitler's Black Shirts the day after he conducted a Sunday worship service in Flossenburg Prison. He refused to walk away from his hurting country even though it cost his life. The world can see through his example — if it will — that there is not enough darkness on this earth to put out the light of one of God's candles.

An Improper Concept of Time

It is not by accident that we are where we are. Our jobs may be hard and our place of employment tough,

---

[6]Ibid., p. 17.

[7]Ibid., pp. 22-24.

[8]Ibid., p. 45.

but like Bonhoeffer, we have been placed to counterbalance evil. The cost for such service to God and our fellowman indeed is great. There will be times when we must remain silent rather than defend our "rights." There will be times when it seems as though we are being taken advantage of or even crucified. Yet the truth of God's Word is that the light will ultimately shatter the darkness.

Millions have chosen, like Bonhoeffer, to face the light and have found the shadows falling behind them. Others, like Nietzsche, have faced the dark only to have the light behind them cast long shadows of fear far into their future. It makes a lot of difference which way one faces. I choose to face the future with hope.

I fear, however, that both the Church and American business suffer from an improper concept of time. The Church, it seems, regards the present as the "nasty now-and-now," a period of trials and trouble through which it must endure while longingly looking forward to the "sweet by-and-by," far from the problems of the present. Business regards the future as "anybody's guess" — and too often the company's economic status as "somebody else's problem." In such an attitude, long-term goals can be sacrificed for short-term profits.

I do not believe this abdication from the present in favor of a future beyond the grave squares with Christ's teachings and with the example lived out in the Early Church. If God had opted for short-term goals, the history of mankind would be much different. God's long-term goal for man and this earth extends over thousands of years.

Christ's life is the example against which we are to measure our own Christian walk.

He said, **Repent: for the kingdom of heaven is at hand** (Matt. 4:17).

He did not say, "As you are powerless to change the world, cloister yourself in your churches away from the world and try to lure sinners into the Church."

Instead, the last words of Jesus to His disciples were:

> . . . **All power is given unto me in heaven and in earth.**
>
> **Go ye therefore, and teach all nations, baptizing them in the name of the Father, and of the Son, and of the Holy Ghost:**
>
> **Teaching them to observe all things whatsoever I have commanded you: and, lo, I am with you alway, even unto the end of the world. Amen**
>
> **Matthew 28:18-20**

Mark records Christ's last words with particular drama:

> **And he said unto them, Go ye into all the world, and preach the gospel to every creature.**
>
> **He that believeth and is baptized shall be saved; but he that believeth not shall be damned.**
>
> **And these signs shall follow them that believe; In my name shall they cast out devils; they shall speak with new tongues;**
>
> **They shall take up serpents; and if they drink any deadly thing, it shall not hurt them; they shall lay hands on the sick, and they shall recover.**

So then after the Lord had spoken unto them, he was received up into heaven, and sat on the right hand of God.

And they went forth, and preached everywhere, the Lord working with them, and confirming the word with signs following. Amen.

Mark 16:15-20

Christians are "Kingdom people" mandated to go out into the world, not retreat. We are to be salt, light, and leaven *in* the world. Salt left in a container is useless; light hidden under a basket burns itself out; leaven left in the package goes stale. Our purpose is not to get people into the Church, but to get the Church into the world! As we practice and proclaim the Kingdom principles of productivity, servanthood, and stewardship, we are **teaching them to observe all things whatsoever I have commanded you** (Matt. 28:20).

Business must be challenged to move beyond the present to plan for the future. Many excellent companies are assuming responsibility for the future, and they are to be applauded. However, others continue to be short-sighted.

Industrial Disinvestment: Cursing the Darkness

Authors Barry Bluestone and Bennett Harrison describe this process in their book, *The Deindustrialization of America*. They said:

Underlying the high rates of unemployment, the sluggish growth in the domestic economy, and the failure to successfully compete in the international market is the deindustrialization of America. By deindustrialization is meant a widespread, systematic disinvestment in the nation's basic productive capacity.

Controversial as it may be, the essential problem with the U. S. economy can be traced to the way capital — in the forms of financial resources and of real plant and equipment — has been diverted from productive investment in our basic national industries into unproductive speculation, mergers and acquisitions, and foreign investment. Left behind are shattered factories, displaced workers, and a newly emerging group of ghost towns.[9]

Bluestone and Harrison claim that capital produced in industry is being taken out of industry and invested into non-industrial and foreign enterprises for short-term gain.

The authors believe, as I have come to believe, that *short-term goals are short-sighted.*

One big problem in the steel industry is the desperate need for modernization. Most steel plants in America are burdened with outdated technology and archaic equipment from the pre-World War II era. On the other hand, foreign steel industry plants were built more recently with newer technology and more efficient equipment. A Japanese plant can produce as much as an American company, faster and less costly.

A conscious effort must be made to plow profits and venture capital back into the steel industry to re-tool and modernize. Short-term sacrifices would have to be made. Shareholders and top-level executives

---

[9] Barry Bluestone and Bennett Harrison, *The Deindustrialization of America* (New York: Basic Books, 1982), p. 26.

would "suffer" relatively frozen returns, but over the long-term, all would benefit.

Economic "Reincarnation" Is Not Working

Amazingly, disinvestment has been proclaimed by many economic analysts as the only way for the economy to grow. Their arguments for this are a throwback of the myth of the Phoenix bird rising from the ashes: a new, better system growing out of the destruction of the old. An example is in 1980 when the U. S. Steel Corporation announced the closing of fourteen mills in eight states. Thirteen thousand workers lost jobs, *but the firm got an $850 million tax break from the federal government.*

A darker side to disinvestment is also described by Bluestone and Harrison:

> There is an enormous amount of evidence that the economic reincarnation process is not working according to the book. Disinvestment is supposed to free labor and capital from relatively unproductive uses in order to put them to work in more productive ones. But very often this is not the case. Virtually all studies of workers who lose their jobs as the result of a plant closing show that a large proportion of the unemployed take years to recover their lost earnings and many never find comparable work at all.

> . . . When the experienced and skilled autoworker in Flint, Michigan, ends up buffing cars in the local car wash, there is a terrible loss of talent and creativity and productivity.

> The cost of disinvestment goes well beyond lost wages and foregone productivity. Workers and their families suffer serious physical and emotional health problems when their employers suddenly shut down operations, and the community as a whole experiences a loss

of revenue needed for supporting police and fire protection, schools, and parks. Entire cities and towns can be brought to the brink of bankruptcy, as has happened in Detroit, Cleveland, and a host of smaller municipalities throughout the industrial Midwest.

The creative destruction process breaks down in an obvious way when deindustrialization produces permanently elevated levels of unemployment. The U. S. Bureau of Economic Analysis has estimated that each one-point increase in the unemployment rate, sustained over an entire year, costs the American economy more than $68 billion in foregone gross national product, $20 billion in federal tax revenues, and $3.3 billion in added expenditures for unemployment benefits, food stamps, and other forms of public aid.[10]

The problem of disinvestment is rooted in dehumanization. Employees seem to be unimportant and expendable in the search for faster and higher profits. This creates a "sweet here-and-now" at a higher cost for workers *and* for a corporation's future.

Dr. Lipke has talked frequently with me about the futility and inhumanity of disinvestment. He sees it as foolhardy for a corporation to disinvest profits from what it does best in order to reinvest speculatively in a business it knows nothing about! He cited Exxon's ill-fated attempt to expand into the office-machine business. The expertise of operating an oil company did not translate to the selling of photocopiers and word processors.

Dr. Lipke feels the bottom line of success in his Gibraltar corporation is not just profit but the future

---

[10]Ibid., pp. 10,11.

welfare of corporation *and* worker. He is working for the future of the firm *and* the future of his employees. Long-range planning goes on constantly. Dr. Lipke's aim is to offer more jobs to the unemployed in western New York state. The focus is on people and community. I see this attitude as the mark of a servant-leader, who is facing the right direction — forward.

Other problems also are deeply disturbing the steel industry. One of these is fragmentation, which is destroying the steel industry. Labor and management have become totally alienated.

Workers often consider management personnel to be heartless, ruled by market forecasts and "the bottom line." Management often looks on labor as faceless statistics or necessary evils.

Conditions in many plants reflect these poor attitudes. Profits went to shareholders first, so plants fell into disrepair. Workers felt little involvement and often allowed the shops to become cluttered and filthy.

Wayne Alderson spoke of this in his book, *Stronger Than Steel:*

> In war, each side knows who the enemy is. But who or what was the enemy at Pittron (Steel)? The goals of both labor and management were, as always, the same. Both wanted higher productivity. Both wanted increased sales. Both wanted better quality of goods and services. Both would welcome a better work atmosphere. But these goals were not being met because they were so busy fighting each other.[11]

---

[11]Wayne Alderson, *Stronger Than Steel* (New York: Harper & Row, 1980), p. 59.

Six Major Problems

If industry is to survive, this adversarialist situation must change. Dr. Lipke set out to change this in his plants. He told me that in his battle to better the climate in the steel industry, he saw six problems:

1. *Dehumanization.*

This developed early with the advent of mass production. In an age of high technology, computers, and robots, the system has further stripped away the personalities of the workers. Employees came and went with many in management unaware of the turnover. Bodies were needed to operate the machinery, and personal involvement between management and labor was considered an unnecessary business practice.

2. *Short-term Vision.*

Concerned more with immediate results in the present, too many companies failed to plan adequately for the future. This was coupled with the refusal to believe statistics about the impact of foreign imports. The attitude of many owners and executives was that, if unprofitability resulted in the future, the business could be sold or shut down and losses written off taxes. Government policies actually encouraged this type of "bail-out."

3. *Misuse of Profit.*

This problem related directly to the short-term vision. The emphasis was on immediate gain at all costs. Plus, rather than profits being directed back into the plants for maintenance, expansion, and modernization, these monies went straight to the shareholders' pockets. As a result, the steel industry failed to install more efficient and cost-effective equipment, and lost out to newer foreign plants operating at cheaper costs.

4. *Failure of Leadership.*

Often some steel executives focused their efforts on their own achievement in climbing corporate ladders. This resulted in bad labor relations. Dr. Lipke set out to put his workers first.

5. *Selfishness.*

Again, this related directly to the problem of leadership. The corporation was seen as existing to be served by employees, customers and the community in which it was located. Nothing was given back, but everything was taken. Instead of seeking ways to help its employees to become more successful, employees often were "locked in" to positions, saving the corporation the trouble of hiring and training to fill changing slots. Hiring focused on outsiders rather than promoting from within. This demoralized the workers, providing no incentive for hard work and improvement in job skills.

6. *Greenfielding.*

Many corporations closed plants in one location and rebuilt a new facility producing the same products in another part of the country. Tax write-off allowances encouraged this, and it was considered less costly to start from scratch than to brownfield, or retool an existing plant. This ignored the devastating impact it leaves on the community.

The primary reason for greenfielding is probably lack of resident ownership. When absentee owners live many miles away from the affected communities, they do not suffer the negative consequences of a move. However, *if communities are allowed more involvement in the ownership of resident businesses, less greenfielding will occur.*

These are the problems Dr. Lipke confronted as he began his involvement in the steel industry. And these are the problems he has tried to address through creative change and commitment. He has been successful, and that in turn, has made Gibraltar one of America's most profitable companies.

While the industrial gurus of America are adopting the Nietzsche philosophy of "cursing the darkness," the entrepreneurial Dr. Lipke has reaffirmed the Bonhoeffer legacy of "lighting a candle." The lighting of a candle is the responsibility of both the Church and its people.

Principle Number Three:
The Dignity of Man

7

Partners for Renewal

As the industrial age progressed, the North American worker became a part of a revolution that made him the most productive person who had ever lived on Planet Earth. Assembly-line ingenuity placed men side by side, working as a team to produce more goods and increase profitability more than earlier generations had thought possible. America consequently became the richest nation in the world.

But in all this progress, Americans failed to recognize an inherent weakness.

First Wave: Agriculture

Previously, man worked primarily in agriculture. He tilled the fields, planted grain, nurtured crops, watched them grow, and then harvested the results of his labors. From the soil he owned or worked with his own hands, he gained produce and profit, fed his own family, and traded the bulk in an open market in order to earn money to improve the quality of his life. He was directly involved in every step of the process. In fact, he made the system happen and made it work.

With the advent of the assembly line, the worker was distanced from the totality, the process, the profits, and the end product. As the Industrial Age advanced, production lines were longer, plants larger, and in most cases, more impersonal.

In earlier days, one man on the line still performed a series of tasks and was close to the end product. He usually knew his co-workers and saw where his effort fit into the overall process, product, and profit. But as the assembly lines grew longer, tasks became specialized, limited, and restricted. Rather than assembling several parts, the worker was reduced to merely inserting a few screws into numbered holes. And as the number of workers on the line also increased dramatically, the climate grew more impersonal.

In Industrial Age, Workers Dehumanized

As industry grew ever larger and more important economically, workers were divorced from management decisions and too often lost sight of the end product because of their specialization and isolation. The process often dehumanized, and many times workers felt they were denied dignity.

Upton Sinclair's bestseller, *The Jungle,* concerning the brutal world of industry, did much to call attention to this tear in the fabric of our working world.

Renewal in America's industrial system must address how to return dignity and worth to the worker.

Renewal Must Return Dignity

Even the most insignificant worker should be made to feel part of the whole. He should feel part of the decision-making processes which directly affect him and his working environment. He should be involved in the total product and should be given a clear view of the company's goals and purposes and of his place in the business.

The worker should be allowed to share in the profits through incentive programs and through having profits redirected back into the plants for improvement and modernization. Renewal must center on the realization that people have value and should be treated with respect, love, and dignity. It is in this role of human dignity that the Church can help greatly in the renewal of industry.

Unhealthy Religion Adds to Confusion

Unhealthy religion can add to the confusion and frustration of disenfranchised workers. If the worker is "preached at" and told how unworthy, low, and sinful he is, probably he will begin to believe it. Often, sermons and hymns describe mankind — even Christians — as "worms" or "wretches."

In one sense this is true, but it must be understood in the proper context. It is true that man is sinful, and in that state is unworthy of the blessings of God, except for salvation. But there is a tremendous difference between being "unworthy" and "worthless." God sees us as "unworthy" but not as "worthless."

In fact, the Bible says mankind has so much *worth* to God that He gave His only begotten Son that we might become what He intends us to be. (John 3:16.) As industry misplaces the value of the person at times, so religion misplaces the image of God inherent in all men.

Man is made in the image of God. (Gen. 1:27.)

Biblical Basis of Dignity

The dignity-of-man principle has good Biblical basis. The psalmist asked:

> **What is man, that thou art mindful of him? and the son of man, that thou visitest him?**
>
> **For thou hast made him a little lower than the angels, and hast crowned him with glory and honour.**
>
> **Thou madest him to have dominion over the works of thy hands; thou has put all things under his feet.**
>
> **Psalm 8:4-6**

The Hebrew word translated here as *angel* is *Elohim*. That really means that man is made just a little lower than God, because *Elohim* most often is translated *God*. Apparently, the King James translators could not believe man was created a little lower than God, so they translated *Elohim* as *angels* in this instance.

In an expanding world, we are tempted to think in an "assembly-line mentality." However, the Bible brings us back to an awareness that we are part of the whole and our individual contributions are priceless. We are God's creation. These commonly asked questions are answered in the Bible: Who am I? How do I fit into the scheme of things? On what do I base my self-esteem?

Even though he is living in sin separated from the mercy of Christ, each person still has inherent value and dignity. He is spiritually redeemable, and God's grace and forgiveness are ever available to him. We see God's respect for man's dignity from the beginning.

Remember what happened in the Garden of Eden when Adam and Eve disobeyed God and ate of the forbidden fruit? God did not totally reject them, humiliate them, or call them "worms." Rather, He called to them by name. In love, He questioned them, to lead them to forgiveness and reconciliation. God moved to heal the breach between Him and them and asked that they accept responsibility for their sin.

When they failed to confess readily, God revealed the natural consequences of their sin which resulted in a much harsher way of life. But at the same time, He gave them clothing, instructed them in how to endure the world's harshness and showed them how to live and find atonement for their sins through sacrifice and devotion.

Although Adam and Eve sinned and had to bear the penalty, in God's eyes they were His children and He loved them. He always was accessible to them. Throughout history, God always has made Himself available to His creation, to His children. That is what the Bible is all about.

Gnosticism

In the second century of Christianity, a sect developed as a twisted mixture of some tenets of Judaism, some Christian teachings, and some Eastern religions. Its main thesis was that spirit was "good" and matter was "evil." The name for this belief came from the Greek word for knowledge, which is *gnosis*.[1]

---

[1]*The New International Dictionary of New Testament Theology, Vol. I.* (Grand Rapids: Zondervan Publishing House, 1967, 1969, 1971), p. 58; and, *Eerdmans' Handbook to the Bible* (Grand Rapids: William B. Eerdmans Publishing Company, 1973), p. 498.

Banned in the fourth century, it went underground to surface in different forms and names through the years. Sometimes called "dualism," it promoted the idea that man has little, if any, intrinsic, value.

Since the physical reality of matter was considered to be totally evil and unredeemable, God could never have created this world or material things — and certainly would never have allowed His Son to be contaminated with the evil of the natural world. The sect developed an entire theology to deal with subordinate beings between God and man who were responsible for material creation. The point, however, is that this view of the body as inherently evil has continued to spill over into Christianity through various scholars such as Thomas Aquinas.

This thinking, of course, disregards the spiritual nature of humans and disregards many passages in the Bible that point to the redemption of spirit and soul, and at the Second Coming, the redemption of the material body into a new transfigured body.

The Bible viewpoint is that man was created in the image of God. This image is marred by sin but not obliterated. Each person bears within himself God's image, and thus is inhabited by the potential for salvation and redemption through Christ. Everyone — saint or sinner — has value in God's eyes. This is clearly evident in the life of Christ as He dealt directly with those who were considered to be the rejects of society.

Reformation Shortcomings

In the sixteenth century, Martin Luther led a reformation of the Church. But, while he dealt with theological imperfections and abuses of the Church, he did not adequately wash out the taint of other philosophies that had crept into the Church over the years. As with most great theologians, he dealt mostly with theological issues. Thus, many modern-day church doctrines still carry the taint of Greek ideologies and Gnosticism.

I feel it is important to understand the philosophical flow of thought. In some cases, the modern American worker has been denied dignity by society and by his church. Thus he has become a number in a faceless society — a "worm" among "worthless" sinners.

A Return of Self-Esteem

I believe a return to American productivity also must involve theological renewal and reevaluation. Robert Schuller calls this a "new theology of self-esteem." In his book, *Self-Esteem: The New Reformation,*[2] he claims we must have a return of dignity. We must once again see value in ourselves and in others.

A basic theme throughout all of Schuller's writings is the need to meet Jesus Christ. Despite the shortcomings, Christ accepts each person as an equal, even though He knows who and what the person is. After that encounter, the person is different. The born again person is able to trust and love. For the first time, he will dare to come out of the bushes and meet his

---

[2]Robert Schuller, *Self-Esteem: The New Reformation* (Dallas: Word Books, 1982).

heavenly Father without fearing rejection. He will dare to accept and experience reconciliation.

Schuller maintains that no psychological or psychiatric therapy can begin to approach the healing power of this religious experience. When a rebellious human who is suffering from insecurity, defensiveness, and feelings of inferiority meets God's unconditional love, he is redeemed into God's family and is ready to think big — as God thinks. Cured of feelings of inferiority by his identification with the family of God, he begins to be released from the negative self-image that keeps him from daring or deserving to think big and beautiful.

Self-esteem will lead to possibility thinking, according to Schuller. When a person is adopted as a child of God, the core of his life changes from shame to self-esteem.

The very wise pastor-evangelist-author gives six steps to gaining a positive self-image through God.

Steps to a Positive Self-Image

1. *Pursue God.*

   Begin by confessing your sin. Be specific, using words that bluntly describe you as you are. "If with all your heart you truly seek him, you shall surely find him . . . ." (Deut. 4:29.)

2. *Reexamine yourself.*

   Ask yourself, "Am I sincerely honest?" Don't play games or pretend. If your problem is doubt, then admit it. For instance, pray, "I thank you, God, that you love me even when my faith is dim, dark, and dreary."

3. *Affirm positively what God is able to do with you.*

In your honesty, do remain affirmative. Negative praying only weakens you. Pray, "I know that you love me anyway. I know that you are waiting eagerly to forgive me for . . . ."

4. *Yield your self-will to God.*

"Not my will, but yours be done, O God." (Luke 22:42.)

5. *Expect positive results.*

Anticipate positive emotions, sense the joy, peace, and faith flowing into you. If you have faith, all things are possible. (Mark 9:23.)

6. *Rejoice!*

In thanking God, be specific, detail your thanks. For example, "Thank you, God, for eyes to see faces of those I love, for ears to hear my favorite music, the sound of a friend's voice on the telephone in the middle of a lonely hour of life."

Schuller then adds, "It's not an accident that the initials of these six steps spell out 'Prayer.' Talk to your heavenly Father often. Remember to entrust your self-image to him."[3]

Spoiled for Intended Use

We do need a reformation in our theology. I see that this theological reformation must include a more adequate definition of sin. Sin primarily is the misuse

---

[3]Robert Schuller, *Self-Love* (Old Tappan: Spire Books, 1975), pp. 145-153.

of God's gifts. We sin when we misuse our time, talents, wealth, property, and bodies, as all of these things are God's gifts. Sex is a gift of God, ordained for expression in marriage. Fornication is a misuse of the gift of sex and thus a sin. Our time, talents, and resources are like fire — properly used to heat a house or process food for survival, or misused to destroy.

In this definition of sin, I think we must go back to perhaps the most familiar salvation scripture of all: John 3:16:

> **For God so loved the world, that he gave his only begotten Son, that whosoever believeth in him should not perish, but have everlasting life.**

The word *perish* means "spoiled for intended use." If fruit perishes, it cannot be used. Goods with a propensity to spoil are called "perishables." I believe sin spoils us to intended use. God has designed each of us with individual talents that can change our world as they are used for God's purposes. Sin diverts the use of these abilities, and thus we are "spoiled." God sent His only begotten Son into the world to keep us from being spoiled for intended use. It is exciting to think that God has programmed people for our troubled time who can be answers to the problems of our world, and we can affect His Kingdom in this world.

The Dignity of the Worker

A policy of industrial renewal must include an emphasis on the dignity and value of the human person. Programs such as employee stock-ownership recognize the proper place of the worker in the scheme of profit- and decision-making. Allowing entrepreneurial leadership places value on the worth of an individual's contribution to his company. Incentive programs properly channel rewards directly to those who have expended the effort worthy of recognition.

When workers are seen as they should be seen — as the most important element in business and industry — and when people are treated with respect, rewarded for their effort, and simply valued for their contribution, management will find that creativity, productivity, and profitability will all flourish.

Every Person a King

Perhaps it is only myth, but I once heard an interesting story about something alleged to have occurred during the French Revolution. King Louis XVI and his queen were condemned by the heads of the revolt to be taken to the guillotine. After they were beheaded, the mob cried for the young prince also to be beheaded, although he was only six years old.

As the child stood on the scaffold trembling, clothed in fine velvet clothing, someone in the mob showed a modicum of compassion.

"Don't kill him," he cried. "He'll just go to heaven, and that's too good for him. Give him to old Meg, the witch. She'll make a sinner out of him, and he'll end up in hell where he belongs."

Soon the old woman began trying to teach the lad vile and profane language, and encouraged the prince to talk and act like a sinner.

But the young lad would determinedly stomp his feet and reply, "I will not say those profane words. I was born to be a king, and a king does not talk like that!"

According to the story, he was never corrupted because of his self-dignity: He knew who he was.

The ultimate purpose of God is to make every person a king — a servant king — ruling from a shared throne of mutual service, love, and compassion. As management returns to the concept of servanthood, and labor returns to roles of servanthood — when each man recognizes the dignity of the other — then industry will be productive and profitable.

Unity in Divergence

As Dr. Lipke and I first talked about these concepts, I sensed we were closer together in thinking than I had anticipated. The industrial world view I had been developing over the past few years was a message I had been preaching in my church.

On the surface, he and I seemed worlds apart. I was a preacher, he an industrialist. He was financially well-off and wore his success well. He lived in relative opulence, surrounded by all the usual visible trappings of wealth well-earned. As the sole owner of one of America's most successful steel companies, he could well afford his hard-earned lifestyle. His financial success was evident.

As we began discussing the circumstances surrounding our coming together, we recognized the almost prophetical nature of our meeting and ascribed it to destiny. Here was a man who had changed the business climate of our city and now had dreams of giving thousands of jobs back to the community.

John Calvin and the City of God

I thought of John Calvin and the influence he had on Geneva, Switzerland. Centuries ago, Calvin's vision was to see a "city of God" built in his homeland. Even today, Geneva has the highest per capita income of any city in the world, four hundred and fifty years after Calvin.[4]

Did Calvin's experience in Geneva and his desire to bring the Kingdom of God to his city and nation have anything to do with the vision Dr. Lipke and I shared, a dream of seeing the great steel industry revitalized, employment restored, and the work ethic reinstituted in society? Were we experiencing the confluence of the city of God with the city of steel, the beginning of the restoration of the Kingdom of God in business and industry?

Confluence of Two Worlds

As we talked and shared our individual dreams, hopes, and visions, our worlds came together as we realized our deep-rooted kinship. We were both natives of the same city, sons of ordinary working men who labored hard to provide for their families. Our dreams were the same, our purposes congruent.

---

[4]Abraham Kuyper, *Lectures on Calvinism* (Grand Rapids: William B. Eerdmans Publishing Company, 1931, 1983); and, Samuel Dunn, compiler, *The Best of John Calvin* (Grand Rapids: Baker Book House, 1981).

Soon it became apparent that Dr. Lipke and I had developed essentially similar philosophical bases on which we had built our lives. We had been schooled in similar philosophies. We shared appreciation for Norman Vincent Peale, Robert Schuller, Zig Ziglar, Doug Wead, and other writers and speakers of like mind. We both knew and understood the basic principles of success and agreed that their ultimate grounding is in the teaching and life of Jesus Christ. We simply wanted to change our city and to change our world.

Following my meeting with Dr. Lipke, my mind was filled with information on the steel industry, its language — blast furnaces, coke ovens, basic oxygen furnaces, hot and cold rolling mills, galvanizing — was a strange new vocabulary for a minister.

Sometimes I wondered if I was getting too far outside what I considered the area of my calling. Yet, I also realized that if I was going to be an effective agent for change, I had to understand the world I was attempting to change. A missionary in a foreign land is useless unless he can learn the language of the natives.

Soon my library began to expand as I added books with titles such as *Megatrends, Revitalizing America: Politics for Prosperity, Stronger Than Steel, A Shopkeeper's Millenium, The Fight Against Shutdowns, The Deindustrialization of America,* and many others.

I became a careful reader of the business section of the newspapers and started to read more business magazines. Soon Dr. Lipke and I could converse comfortably, not only about God's Kingdom principles, but I could hold my own in a conversation on business and industry.

Men of God Called to Rebuild the Walls

Many of the books and articles I read provided powerful arguments against rebuilding the industries of America. Many claimed we must deindustrialize and give the basic industries over to other developing nations. They suggested we become an information society, providing information and services to the developing nations who will operate basic industries. Yet everything within me rebels against this concept.

While the information sector of our society naturally will expand, we cannot sacrifice our basic industries. We cannot succumb to the danger of being overly dependent on other nations for our goods and products.

We cannot ignore the plight of the swelling ranks of unemployed workers in America. Everyone cannot fit into the information network. I believe it is our responsibility before God to put people back to work in industry, which they have served for so long. Industry is vital to the strength and security of our nation.

Was it not a moral and spiritual question that brought about the existence of America in the first place? Was it not the revival under Charles Finney that pricked the conscience of men and eventually resulted in the abolishment of slavery and other social inequities? Is it possible that God is calling men of God all across America into the task of rebuilding the

crumbling walls of American business and industry?
I believe so.

Principle Number Four:
Non-Absentee Landlords

8

Rehumanizing Industry: Practical Applications

The helicopter banked sharply to the right, and I peered past Ken Lipke as we bounced over the Bethlehem Steel plant. White clouds of smoke billowed upward, giving some evidence steel was still being produced. It was a small sign of life in an otherwise dead plant.

Perhaps, I thought, all is not lost. If somehow our problems could be isolated and addressed, then appropriate solutions could be found, and the steel plant and our city could thrive again. Ken and I circled the dying plant with the helicopter's blade thumping loudly above us as I started to ponder.

Give the Fig Tree Another Chance

What, specifically — if anything — does the Word say, I wondered, about a steel plant or industry that becomes nonproductive? Certainly this plant, among others, was unprofitable. My mind drifted back to a parable Jesus told:

Then he used this illustration:

"A man planted a fig tree in his garden and came again and again to see if he could find any fruit on it, but he was always disappointed. Finally he told his gardener to cut it down. 'I've waited three years and there hasn't been a single fig!' he said. 'Why bother

with it any longer? It's taking up space we can use for something else.'

" 'Give it one more chance,' the gardener answered. 'Leave it another year, and I'll give it special attention and plenty of fertilizer. If we get figs next year, fine; if not, I'll cut it down.' "

Luke 13:6-9 TLB

Story of the Profitable Servants

From my theological background, I knew keenly that God demands profitability from each life. There are serious consequences, if we fail to be productive. Perhaps the most emphatic of these parables on productivity is a very well-known one:

"Again, the Kingdom of Heaven can be illustrated by the story of a man going into another country, who called together his servants and loaned them money to invest for him while he was gone.

"He gave $5,000 to one, $2,000 to another, and $1,000 to the last — dividing it in proportion to their abilities — and then left on his trip. The man who received the $5,000 began immediately to buy and sell with it and soon earned another $5,000. The man with $2,000 went right to work, too, and earned another $2,000.

"But the man who received the $1,000 dug a hole in the ground and hid the money for safekeeping.

"After a long time their master returned from his trip and called them to him to account for his money. The man to whom he had entrusted the $5,000 brought him $10,000.

"His master praised him for good work. 'You have been faithful in handling this small amount,' he told him, 'so now I will give you many more responsibilities. Begin the joyous tasks I have assigned to you.'

"Next came the man who had received the $2,000, with the report, 'Sir, you gave me $2,000 to use, and I have doubled it.'

" 'Good work,' his master said. 'You are a good and faithful servant. You have been faithful over this small amount, so now I will give you much more.'

"Then the man with the $1,000 came and said, 'Sir, I knew you were a hard man, and I was afraid you would rob me of what I earned, so I hid your money in the earth and here it is!'

"But his master replied, 'Wicked man! Lazy slave! Since you knew I would demand your profit, you should at least have put my money into the bank so I could have some interest. Take the money from this man and give it to the man with the $10,000. For the man who uses well what he is given shall be given more, and he shall have abundance. But from the man who is unfaithful, even what little responsibility he has shall be taken from him. And throw the useless servant out into outer darkness: there shall be weeping and gnashing of teeth.' "

Matthew 25:14-30 TLB

The Personal Touch

Obviously, God demands profitability, and that led me to ask myself another searching question. Why was Dr. Lipke's steel plant profitable while others were failing? Here was a man who had, during a recent severe recession, been at the helm of one of the twenty-five out of four thousand steel companies that had produced a profit.

What made the difference? His company had to compete in the same market as those other steel companies that had been "hurt" by recession and foreign steel. What was the single ingredient, or perhaps ingredients, that made the difference? In just a few moments, I was to witness one answer to my question.

We flew over Lake Erie and landed on the famed old estate now owned by Gibraltar Steel. Two red all-terrain vehicles met us at the heliport, and we drove through the magnificent acreage. It was a special tour, and we climbed to the top of an unused water tower in the middle of the property to look over the beautiful grounds. Later, we walked to where some men were repairing a porch on one of the estate's buildings.

The carpenters, wet with perspiration from their labor, stopped as we approached. Ken introduced me to each man by his full name. He knew them well and related to me briefly how each had come to work for him. It was obvious they respected him, and that he respected them. What amazed me was that he knew so many details about each of the workers we met. I began to see they were important to him — who they were, not just what they did.

Here was a key: the difference I was seeking.

Dr. Lipke employed more than 1,200 people in his steel plants alone. Yet each one mattered to him. He cared about his people, and he cared about his community.

He says, "The measure of any company is its people."

If employees become statistics on a report from a plant an employer may never visit, then it is almost too simple and too easy to lay off thousands of them. They begin to feel like numbers and do not give their best in ideas and effort to the company. Profitability is then diminished.

There is one basic "ingredient" that must be included in any business mix to assure even minor success! Brilliant people and exceptional business savvy are definite pluses, but many companies have succeeded without these, operating strictly on simple common sense and "flying-by-the-seat-of-the-pants" management.

A Common Goal Is Needed

Extensive capital and available credit are other essentials for business endeavors. Yet there exist many stories of success where a business was literally started from nothing, with nothing, and made millions. In all cases of successful businesses, however, there is a common thread: the people in that business wanted it desperately to succeed. With people power, the impossible often becomes possible. I found my new friend, Ken Lipke, had tapped into this truth.

Good businesses cannot be established on the bent backs of hard-working employees. When successes come, the employees who made that success cannot be taken for granted, abused, and ignored. Quality attention and consideration must be given to the people who make the products and present them on the marketplace.

I learned that when Dr. Lipke took over Gibraltar Steel the workers had felt for several years their needs had been ignored. The work environment had become emotionally sterile and somewhat dehumanized. Management practice precluded friendships with employees, and there were exaggerated fears of being exploited.

In reaction, unions restricted management and labor cooperation, complaining on one hand that management did not do enough for labor, and on the other, demanding in their contracts extreme limits on what could be done. Management and labor looked on each other with suspicion, hostility, and animosity. There was little sense of respect and each side seemed to deny dignity to the other. Yet, it all turned around, and an unprofitable steel plant shortly began to make money.

The turnaround started with management insisting on the individual dignity of the working man.

Dr. Lipke began to visit each shift, and to learn each worker's dreams and families. He cleaned up and modernized the working facilities, making tasks easier and more enjoyable to perform. He talked often with employees and remembered their anniversaries and birthdays. He provided on-going training programs and advanced education opportunities for them. He began promoting from within, rather than reaching out into the marketplace for "new talent." They began to feel better about themselves and then began to perform better. Profits resulted. They took pride in their work and their products. They were more than machines.

Dr. Lipke was working out the Biblical view of man in the market place. The Bible sees every person on earth as possessing inherent dignity and value, because he is in God's image. Regardless of whether that person believes in God, he still bears the mark of God in his life. Thus no man has the right to devalue another, to deny another dignity and self-esteem. No one is more or less valuable than anyone else.

Work Designated by God

A second Biblical concept is that the *work ethic* was not something created by the Puritans to keep people from an excessive pursuit of pleasure, but it was given by God. Work was ordained in the garden by God before sin ever corrupted this world. God worked in creating the heavens, earth, man, and beasts. Since His image is ingrained in man, it is only natural that man work.

A third Bible principle deals with the purpose of work. Man is commissioned to care for the earth, to use and protect its resources. Everything is under man's "dominion" and care, and all is considered good. Matter is neither good nor evil but is to be used as "good" in the hands of men bringing the greatest good to this earth.

Finally, the result of man's labor is to be fruitful and multiply. This means to produce, reproduce, replenish, and fill the earth with profitability. The Bible gives dignity, purpose, and power to man, whether he is a corporate president or one who digs a ditch. Each has his purpose, and each is ordained by God.

A business must be built around the value of people and recognizing their needs. Profitability demands the work environment to be comfortable, clean, and conducive for positive attitudes. A physical plant must reflect the dignity of the people it will house. There must be adequate restrooms, break and lunch areas located away from machinery, adequate lighting, cooling, and heating. There should be noise-limiting structures and devices to create a physical environment for people, rather than people being forced to adapt to an environment made for machines.

Mutual Returns

Modern management emphasizes that profitability also depends on the way people are treated and how they are allowed to treat each other. Peters and Waterman say, in *In Search of Excellence:*

> Our findings were a pleasant surprise. The project showed, more clearly than could have been hoped for, that the excellent companies were, above all, brilliant on the basics. Tools didn't substitute for thinking. Intellect didn't overpower wisdom. Analysis didn't impede action. Rather, these companies worked hard to keep things simple in a complex world. They persisted. They insisted on top quality. They fawned over their customers. They listened to their employees and treated them like adults. They allowed their innovative produce and service "champions" long tethers. They allowed some chaos in return for quick action and regular experimentation.[1]

Good management really is rather simple: *It simply means to treat people as equal human beings, not as machines or slaves.*

---

[1]Copyright © 1982 by Thomas J. Peters and Robert H. Waterman, Jr. Reprinted from *In Search of Excellence* by Harper & Row, Publishers, Inc.

Benefits at Gibraltar

Employers have a greater responsibility in being used by God since they serve as channels through which their employees can be blessed and sustained. If an employer refuses to remunerate an employee for his work, where else is the employee to go to have his needs met? If working harder and producing more does not yield a proportionately greater reward, how is the employee supposed to care for himself and his family?

Christ said, **For unto whomsoever much is given, of him shall be much required: and to whom men have committed much, of him they will ask more** (Luke 12:48). Management has been given much, and inherent in that position as an employer is the obligation to employees.

As I got to know Dr. Lipke and learn of his management policies, I discovered there are three levels of humanizing at Gibraltar Steel. These are directed first to the employee, then the customer, and finally, to the community.

One striking practice of Dr. Lipke's company is his insistence on getting to know each individual who works at Gibraltar Steel. When he first took over the company, he had the employees wear their names on their hard hats, so he could more quickly learn who they were by name. Now names are no longer on their hats, but he knows his people. He listens to their ideas and problems. Dr. Lipke firmly believes his business is not to build a big company but to build big people.

Every employee at Gibraltar receives a Christmas card and a birthday card. They are given fruit baskets, awards, and special gifts. Parties and get-togethers are regular events conducted like mini-galas. Nothing is done cheaply for the employees.

Dr. Lipke says, "At our social gatherings, you cannot tell the cleaning people from the executives. I remember one couple who once were afraid to come to our parties. They felt uncomfortable associating with the bosses on a social level. (I find that attitude common in many American businesses.) It took this couple five years, but finally, they began coming to our parties, and to their surprise, felt accepted and appreciated."

A full-range benefit plan is available for all employees, and a regular fitness program is maintained. One of Dr. Lipke's personal crusades is to encourage smokers to quit the habit, and the only pressure he applies is genuine concern and gentle persuasion. Often, he will stop and spend several minutes discussing with an employee the dangers of smoking. They know he is concerned for their health and well-being. Even if they continue to smoke, they are still respected and rewarded for their contribution to the company.

Dr. Lipke has spent years developing a complex, multilayered system of rewards that opens benefits to everyone at Gibraltar, based on both team accomplishment and individual effort. Unlike simple systems that reward both those who expend effort and those who do not, his system recognizes merit in spite of seniority or rank.

Promotions From Within

At Gibraltar, rising to one's level of competence and ability is considered the norm, and promotions are

encouraged within the company. In 1965, Joe Rosenecker came to work at Gibraltar part-time in a position
one step above the janitor. In 1967, he was moved into
an inside sales position, and then in 1973, he was given
an opportunity at outside sales. In 1974, he was named
director of purchasing, and the following year he was
promoted to vice president of sales. In 1978, he was
promoted again — to executive vice president.

On July 1, 1970, Gibraltar Steel celebrated its 25th
anniversary, a day of emotion and pride, especially for
Rosenecker. As he read his morning newspaper that
day, he was in for a big, but joyful, surprise. The
opening paragraphs of the news story informed him
that he had been named president of the company
where he began as a mill helper fourteen years before.

Rather than go outside the company for a new
president, Dr. Lipke had reached inside for a qualified
and loyal employee. He says, "I get a lot of pride
out of helping people reach their potential." He has
a plaque outside his office that summarizes this
philosophy: "There is always room at the top."

Dr. Lipke believes the "world of opportunity"
should extend not only to his employees but also to
his customers. He believes marketing should involve
seeking out what products are needed now and planning for products to be needed in the future. He shuns
fast profit at the expense of customers.

Early in his efforts of turning Gibraltar into a
profitable company, he approached suppliers with an
unusual offer. He surveyed each one to find which of
their products used by Gibraltar brought the supplier

the most profit. Then, those were the products he bought!

Proposed changes are scrutinized and not enacted unless they are absolutely necessary. When price increases are necessary, the salesmen honestly and carefully explain all the factors involved to their customers. Dr. Lipke believes an almost adversarial position is needed between the sales and production departments to always give the best break to the customer.

Serving the Community

Dr. Lipke and his company show concern for the community. He established several services to benefit his community and contributes a great deal to area arts and entertainment activities. He also frequently brings in well-known speakers for various civic groups. His aim is to establish a better quality of life for his community as well as for his employees.

He says, "Long ago, I ceased doing things for money. Now I do them because my heart goes out to the needs of my community. There are ten thousand unemployed steelworkers in this area. If we were to put a 'Help Wanted' sign out for a handful of jobs, we would have all of those unemployed lined up outside our offices."

This bothers him. He looks at his community and sees the devastation left behind in steel's demise. Steelworkers are unemployed, but so are are workers in other businesses that feel the ripple effect of a massively depressed economy. Business can and should be profitable. Some people may be surprised, but the Bible gives the foundation stones for building a successful business.

The fig tree of industry, although now unprofitable (unfruitful), can be fertilized with the restoration of dignity to the worker and again can produce fruit.

Model Two Has Similar Concerns, Attitudes

At M. Cardone Industries, Inc., both in the office and in the various plants (seventeen in Philadelphia and a distribution center in Los Angeles and one in Houston), the entire atmosphere is one of concern and caring. As executives walk among the employees, they address many by name — asking specific questions about their families or commenting on the work in progress.

Michael Cardone, Jr., chief executive officer, said, "We don't believe in management and labor. We prefer to call it leadership. There is nobody in this business who is any more important than the guy on the line. We just have different jobs. I'm called to a different work than he is, but I am no more important. We are all God's children. Nobody is more important than the other in God's sight."

This belief, or philosophy of management, is evident in the way employees are promoted into leadership, or executive, positions. Cardone listed seven members of his top management team who were promoted up through the ranks. Some started work for the company right out of high school and some after college. One man worked part time while attending Oral Roberts University, then moved into a full-time job.

135

"I think that is scriptural," Cardone said, "Jesus did not choose the greatly educated ministers of the day. They were the worst problems that He had. He picked lay people and trained them according to His way."

Not only do Cardone employees have the opportunity to write directly to the company president, who personally replies to each one, but they can recommend other people whom they know as prospective employees. To assist them in progressing, many production incentive programs are available, both for teams and for individuals, with tangible rewards for those who show improvement.

Each week, one of the departments has a special luncheon which Michael Jr. attends to chat with those employees and get their ideas. Building up self-esteem is one of the top concerns of Cardone Industries. This is done through personal recognition.

"Many people go through a lifetime never being applauded, never being a winner, never being on the winning team," one company officer noted. "Self-esteem is important. That is self-image, and as Michael has said, we are all God's children, and we want to treat each other in that manner. That is the key in what we're doing."

Employees are motivated to grow intellectually, socially, and spiritually through a wide variety of company programs: a family recreation center, camp for employees' children, benevolence fund, college scholarship fund, youth activities, Pioneer Girls, Royal Rangers, New Life Center Choirs, and "Women as One" organization for employees' wives.

Employee seminars also are sponsored in home maintenance, income tax preparation, and similar subjects.

Concern for Families

A concern for the families of the almost 1,000 employees is also shown. In addition to company-wide picnics and carnivals — with the company picking up most of the bill — a program is presented once a week in a "fun arcade." These evenings, which are open to all employees' children and their friends, consist of time in the arcade, an inspirational period, and pizza and soda pop, compliments of the company.

Many youth and employee sports activities are sponsored by the firm, such as softball, soccer, basketball, volleyball, golf, and tennis.

Cardone emphasized their aim of ministering to, or being concerned about, the entire family. This is essential, particularly because such a large percentage of the employees are new to Western ways.

He said, "The kids get caught up all too quickly in the drug culture. Parents don't know what is going on, but they get a new car and this and that, then find they have lost their children. That's why we feel we need to do something with those kids to try to show them there is a better way."

Cultural events are held for all ethnic groups, as each group has different holidays. For example, each has a different New Year's day. A Christmas party for handicapped children and disabled parents held in recent years has drawn more than five hundred in attendance.

One of his executives said, "There is another valuable Biblical truth involved here. When you minister to the entire family and people can come to work with their minds at peace, they will be able to produce more. Our philosophy has been to care about their children, to try to minister to them any way we can. And we have set up some unique programs.

"We send the children to camp in the summer. We have contests and programs designed for children so the young people can have a sense of participation in what their parents do. We send them to ball games, and as Michael (Cardone) said, it shows our concern, helps the parents, and creates a better working environment. That is one of the things we strive for, as we think a good working environment is very important."

Spiritual Life Emphasized

Due to their religious convictions, the Cardones — a father-and-son team — have hired many Third World natives as employees: refugees from Laos, Pakistan, Cambodia, Burma, Colombia, and so forth.

Cardone said, "Because of their age, for some of them this is the first job they ever really have had. Their countries fell apart before they entered the job market. Many companies would not even allow them to apply for jobs, as they speak limited English. We help them learn the language of their new country by providing language classes."

Although the Cardones are deeply religious people, they do not ask about the religion of their employees.

"All we want is to show the love of Jesus, not through our words but through our actions," according to Michael Cardone Jr.

He said "I think one of the greatest things we can do is provide these newcomers to our shores with a job. It is a tangible way to let them know we care about them."

The company also sponsors church services, complete with robed choirs, in its chapel in the main office building. Many noted ministers have been invited to speak to the employees. The company also has been the birthplace of several ethnic chapel services, Bible fellowships, and even churches — including Portuguese, Spanish, and Italian.

Michael Cardone Sr. is one of the recipients of the Churchman of the Year award from the Assembly of God Graduate School in Springfield, Missouri, in recognition of his ministries and missionary projects.

One of the company's mottoes is, "Together we can work wonders."

Another is, "Excellent in all things, and in all things, glory to God."

Absentee Ownership

Absentee ownership never has the same impact as resident ownership. Dr. Lipke lives in and for his community.

He says, "When you own something, you are going to take very good care of it. One expends less effort on rental property, especially one where you don't live, than on a home you own. I am vitally interested in my company and its success because I live in this community. My roots are here. When I share that sense of ownership with my people through profit, they care more for Gibraltar. In a very real sense, the company is theirs as much as mine. We share responsibilities and profits."

Workers have the best equipment the company can afford and the most modern technology available. Everything is well-maintained with no shortcuts to quality. Much of the sense of well-being experienced by the workers comes from the knowledge that Gibraltar will never "greenfield" by relocating its operations elsewhere.

"Why do some companies 'greenfield'?" Dr. Lipke was asked.

He answered, "We have all the skilled labor we need right here in Buffalo. We have all the facilities we need. We have a community in western New York that has grown up with steelmaking, understands it, and knows how to live with it. The big steel companies claim it is too expensive to modernize their plants here, yet it will cost at least $10 billion to relocate and less than $1 billion to "brownfield" their existing plants and stay here.

"I believe this happens because government has created too many policies offering what amounts to incentives for companies to move a plant from one place to another. Probably one of the most significant causes for the demise of American industry is the interference of a government that really doesn't understand industry."

Dr. Lipke believes it is critical for companies to be owned by those who live in the community where the plants are located. Without resident ownership, it becomes too easy for corporations to shut plants down.

Principle Number Five:
The Law of Money — Profits

9

Profit Is Not a Four-Letter Word: Christian Attitudes Toward Money

Businessman David Nelson says, *"Profit* is not a four-letter word — but *loss* is!"

I know he is right. Money . . . profit . . . wealth . . . what comes to mind when one hears these words? For some in the Church, the connotation is often a negative one. In some believers, there seems to exist a kind of schizophrenic love/hate attitude toward wealth. Frequently the "anti-money" position prevails. Is this correct? Should the Christian shun money and avoid wealth? I believe not. In the Bible, I see scriptures that command profitability, but also I see a warning:

> **No man can serve two masters: for either he will hate the one, and love the other; or else he will hold to the one, and despise the other. Ye cannot serve God and mammon** [money].
>
> **Matthew 6:24**

Without profits, there would be no business or benefits to workers. Yet it is understood that profits come from serving the needs of others. Long-term profits are not possible at the expense of workers, customers, and communities. At Gibraltar Steel, profits are primary, but serving the needs of others is how the company exists. This servant mentality is borne out in how Ken Lipke uses company earnings and is expressed in his *five-point philosophy of profit:*

A company must earn a profit, reinvest and reduce debt, invest in retirement, enhance the community, and share with employees.

Point One:
A Company Must Earn a Profit

Dr. Lipke says, "I have a lot of ideas on how to improve and expand my business, and I have a great desire to see my people prosper, but I also know that, if I own a company that doesn't have as its first concern the making of a profit, I won't be able to put any of my ideas into effect or do anything to help my people. A bankrupt company can never make donations to the employees or community. Only profitable companies survive, expand, and benefit."

Point Two:
Reinvest in the Company and Reduce Debt

Since survival of the company is tied to profitability, Dr. Lipke believes profits must first of all be applied to reducing debts of the company. He believes excessive outstanding debts stand as a constant threat to his company's well-being and lead to disaster. He also sees that periodic debt is at times necessary. Emergency situations or an exceptional opportunity requiring extra capital are two good reasons for debt. But great care must be taken to insure the continual welfare of the organization by keeping it free of excessive debt and interest payments.

The company must reinvest in its own facility in maintenance and modernization to ensure continuing viability. When Dr. Lipke first took over, finances were tight. To make the business work, the "executive level" personnel had to sacrifice in salaries as the company sought to recover. Many times in the beginning, he relates, he and his partner were not paid as much as the garbage man! But profits were plowed back into the company, and things did turn around.

Dr. Lipke says, "Companies that don't keep pace with technology and the advances being made in modern thinking and business practices will die."

The steel industry is rife with examples where this has occurred. At times, profits have been siphoned from facilities into other endeavors, leaving the industry unable to keep up with innovative competition. Plants were closed, devastating communities and displacing families dependent on them.

Gibraltar recently completed a $4 million modernization project in one of its five plants and has broken ground for another $1.6 million addition.

Dr. Lipke says, "You can have the greatest people in the world, and they can survive with poor tools for awhile. But the cost of that kind of survival is inevitably too great. Our attitude is that we want to have the best people, give them the best tools, housed in the best facility. It is amazing how a clean workplace enhances a person's self-worth, and thus, profitability."

Point Three: Retirement Investment

Every company has a responsibility to invest in the retirement and future of its employees. Some employees give their entire lives working for a single company. They need to be assured their pensions are secure because of careful planning and concern by the company. Ken Lipke personally knows the disappointment of bad retirement planning.

He says, "My father worked for a steel company for forty years, only to end up with a $38-a-month pension. I feel the company disregarded the future of the worker to support the profits of the moment. I think that's unfair."

At Gibraltar, he has attempted to create advantages to increase the income generated within the profit-sharing plans, tax deferral programs, and other benefits to guarantee workers will have substantial resources when they retire. He takes into consideration cost-of-living increases and other variables. Gibraltar also offers extensive help to the employees for their own financial planning and works hard to protect the future well-being of its employees.

He says, "When our people have worked and kept our company profitable through their attitudes and efforts, when they retire, we want to be there for them, just as they have been here for us."

He believes they must be respected for their efforts, then honored and cared for after they have left the job.

Point Four:
Enhancing the Community

The company has a responsibility to invest in the future and in the quality of life of the community in which it is located. The company depends on the community to provide its employees. Each industry has a great effect on the physical environment. This is true particularly with steel plants and other intensive industries. The company must assume a marked concern to not adversely affect the environment in air, noise, and water pollution. A company also should keep its property as attractive and well cared for as possible.

Since the success of the company is dependent somewhat on the success of the community, the industry should contribute to the welfare of that community. Understanding this principle, Dr. Lipke makes sure Gibraltar contributes regularly to churches, the United Fund, and other benevolent organizations in Buffalo.

Point Five:
Sharing Blessings With Employees

A company also should distribute its profits to its employees in a determined fashion. Basic benefits always are available to employees, but Dr. Lipke believes his obligation goes farther — to providing added benefits, increased salaries, and special rewards.

Dr. Lipke devised a seven-tiered system of benefits and rewards that distributes bonuses to everyone at all levels within the company. He then breaks down additional benefits to divisions, teams within divisions, and individuals within teams. Individuals are recognized based on a combination of division, team, and individual performance, and individuals are recognized based on a combination of team and individual merit. Finally, individuals are recognized based on overall outstanding performance, regardless of their team or division's performance.

One of the key ingredients in Dr. Lipke's system is its emphasis on merit over seniority or position. Both those who have been with the company over a long term and the new employee are motivated to work hard and are open to receive bonuses.

Similar recognition is given by Cardone Industries, which has an incentive program to increase the units per person. The firm also has different teams in the individual plants, and bonuses are given to the winning team. There are quota busters and bonuses, as well as cash safety prizes and bonuses for ideas.

Profit Principles and Future Goals

American industry and business are in desperate need of renewal and most would agree the basic problems are: 1) Workers' loss of dignity, 2) the need of rehumanizing the workplace, 3) a seeming lack of concern for the future and an overemphasis on short-term profits, 4) a misuse of profits through disinvestment, 5) self-serving leadership, and 6) burdening communities by absentee landlords who are not integrated into the local community.

Before meeting Dr. Lipke, I knew the theological demands for Christians to be involved in this world, bringing hope and renewal to the workplace. However, he showed me how these principles work in attitude and philosophy. Here are concrete examples, and although Gibraltar is not perfect, it can stand as a model of how to achieve renewal in the workplace.

Dr. Lipke says, however, "I have never had money as one of my goals. As Henry Ford said, 'Money is merely a commodity, one of the ingredients to accomplishment.' Working for money is a dead end."

What next? Dr. Lipke has brought renewal to Gibraltar, but he is not done. Being a dreamer as well as a doer, he sees problems that still exist in his community, and he is driven to help.

He says, "I believe American business can be revitalized. Industry is still breathing. Some may think of it as a terminal case, but even terminally ill patients have hope, very real hope."

About the Bethlehem Steel plant that he once hoped to revitalize, he says, "If there is life left, yes, anything can be saved. Even now, there may be a flicker of life and hope. If you don't try, death is inevitable. If there is still life, I have to try. A person can have all the right information, wonderful plans, and great financial backing, but it is all wasted until he applies it in action to the situation. You must try before you can succeed."

Dr. Lipke believes all the information needed for revitalization is in the Bible, but he also believes God works *through* man. God's Word is powerless, he says, unless we allow it to work through us. He acknowledges that success only comes through the help of God. It would take many like him to turn the nation back to profitability, productivity, and strength, but it can happen. Business is not intended just to make the "rich richer," but in order that more people may be served.

Jesus was right! Money should be taken from the unprofitable servant and given to the profitable, so the profitable can provide employment to more people and services and products to an ever-expanding market.

Cardone's Four-Fold Pledge

M. Cardone Industries has as its *four-fold pledge:* "to honor God in all we do, help people develop, pursue excellence, and grow profitably."

"Our work is our witness," Michael Cardone Jr. notes. "We show people the love of Christ through having a good product, good service, and good availability, and by providing steady employment and paying our bills. These are the standards by which the world looks at a company. If we don't measure up, then we're not doing what we were called to do.

"I was an undergraduate at Oral Roberts University, and Oral's vision for his students — his mandate — was to train students to take His light where His light was dim, and His voice where His voice is not heard. I feel called to that ministry, in that — in our business world — we are called to *be* lights and to *show* the Light, not to preach it. We witness through our work. That is the greatest witness we can have, by being an outstanding example in the business community."

Profit is not a four-letter word.
It is an ingredient to rehumanize industry.

Principle Number Six:
The Law of Creativity

10

Who Is an Entrepreneur?

Who is the entrepreneur? What makes an entrepreneur tick? Can anyone be an entrepreneur, or is it a God-given gift?

To hear what former President Ronald Reagan spoke, one would think we could become a nation of entrepreneurial people. Can we? Exactly what was the President talking about anyway?

If an entrepreneur is anything at all, he is a *person who lives out, or fulfills, the dreams born in the spirit man inside of him.* While others have dreams that lie dormant, the entrepreneur believes and acts upon the dreams that God has given him.

Although pastor of a church, I can be more accurately described as an entrepreneur. The church I pastor, the Buffalo School of the Bible, the Association of Church-centered Bible Schools with more than one hundred schools, the television ministry, and the business endeavors with which I am involved show the aspect of entrepreneurship. Even this book is the result of an entrepreneurial inclination in my nature.

I learned to dream early in my life. I was a little boy in the middle of the 1930s when the worst of the depression had passed. News of the war in Europe was claiming headlines and dominating the radio news broadcasts. But at that time, the days of my family were filled with renewed joy and hope. A brand new car sat in our driveway. It was only a simple Ford V8-60 horsepower purchased at the end of the model year, but as far as we were concerned, it was a limousine. A few other simple luxuries also began to fill the house, making my mother's life a little easier.

I was in the third grade. Each day when our teacher dismissed class, we all ran screaming out the school doors. I would run all the way home up Emery Road, and my mother always was waiting for me at the door of the house.

"Never Stop Dreaming"

"Tommy," my mother said to me one day when I got home, "let's walk up to Emery Park before it gets dark. Okay?"

I agreed readily, because I loved Emery Park and the playgrounds. We walked up to the park, and I played happily for some time. Then just before twilight, I tired of the swings. As the lowering sun shone brightly on the varicolored autumn trees, Mom and I walked home kicking the fallen leaves into the air. Finally, both exhausted, we lay down in the grass, looking straight up at the crisp blue sky, filled with a multitude of billowy white clouds.

"What do you see?" she asked.

I described trains, boats, houses, castles, and a score of other objects. As we dreamed together, we talked of taking one of those "ships" to a distant land or one of those "trains" to a faraway city. We "dreamed."

Suddenly, Mother turned to me and said, "Tommy, never stop dreaming!"

Words I will never forget, words that have created an exciting life for me throughout these many years. The seemingly "fantasy" world of the dream has become a reality in my life. Today, I do the things I only dreamed about yesterday.

A few days ago, I drove up that same country road, got out of my car, walked over to that same soft grass where Mom and I had played earlier. Above, the clouds sailed by quietly just as they had then, but there was a difference — Mom died thirty-three years ago. And I still miss her.

Tears filled my eyes as I heard her say again, "Tommy, never stop dreaming."

And I haven't!

That, to me, is the entrepreneur: the person who dreams, who will "let go and let God" speak to him and then work through him to create the dream God has placed in his heart. I remember sitting in the beautiful conference room at Gibraltar Steel with a group of preachers once.

Dr. Lipke sat on the side of the desk and said, "You think this is a steel plant. It is not. What you are seeing today is in reality a dream."

And, of course, that is exactly what our two model industries really are, along with many others like them — dreams born in the hearts of men.

Revival of Entrepreneurship

As Daniel had creative ideas that solved the problems of Babylon, so God will put creative ideas in the hearts of His entrepreneurs today, ideas that can change the business community of this nation. I believe one of the greatest secrets to rebuilding the economic walls of America is a coming revival of entrepreneurship. A new generation of "dreamers" is here. God is raising up His "Josephs" in our nation for this day.

Napoleon said, "Imagination rules the world." Right, Napoleon! It always has and always will. In fact, this very universe was once only an "idea" in the imagination of God. Perhaps someone reading this book right now will be used by God in the Creator's revival of entrepreneurial leadership.

Ideas change the world. When President Franklin D. Roosevelt called Henry Kaiser into his office to tell him we were losing World War II because we did not have enough merchant ships, Kaiser asked the President why Bethlehem or other shipbuilders could not meet the need.

President Roosevelt replied, "They say it can't be done."

Kaiser replied, "If it can't be done, then I will do it!"

History records that he did it. But do you know how? The ships were constructed on an assembly line with the goal of making hundreds of vessels each year. The secret of the process was a weld that would hold them together as they were moved and turned right-side-up after assembly. I always believed this secret must have come from God. Therefore, I thought Henry Kaiser must have been a Christian, since truly great creativity is a product of the Holy Spirit. *Great ideas always come from God.*

One day I had lunch with the son of Christian industrialist R. G. LeTourneau. Knowing Mr. LeTourneau had been a friend of Kaiser, I asked the son if his father had led Mr. Kaiser to Christ.

"Not to my knowledge, although they often talked about God."

I then shared my question as to the creativity behind the process of the weld.

Richard LeTourneau's eyes lit up, as he said, "Oh, the weld! That is an interesting story. My father was in prayer one night, and the idea of that weld came to him in prayer. He shared the secret God had given him with Mr. Kaiser. That idea was the secret of the Liberty and Victory ships of World War II."

Yes, truly great ideas come from God. Henry Kaiser's secret weld really *had* come from God.

Dr. Oral Roberts states that all of his great ideas have come to him as he has spoken in tongues and interpreted it back in English. The ideas for buildings, for Oral Roberts University, and for the City of Faith all came in the very same way.

I know in my own life that all the successful ideas that I have ever turned into reality have come through prayer and through "letting go and letting God" speak to me and work through me. One cannot help but link the revival of interest in the Holy Spirit with the revival of entrepreneurship. Spiritual renewal will make Josephs and Daniels for our generation.

The 23rd Psalm: A Success Story

The two industries used as models in this book are excellent examples of entrepreneurial dreaming.

Dr. Lipke attributes all his success to the advice of a mentor many years ago, who said, "Ken, 'let go and let God.' "

Early every morning, he prays the 23rd Psalm in this manner:

The Lord is my shepherd — *guidance.*

I shall not want — *abundance.*

He maketh me to lie down in green pastures — *opportunity.*

He leadeth me beside the still waters — *peace.*

He restoreth my soul — *faith.*

He leadeth me in the paths of righteousness for his name's sake — *conscience.*

Yea, though I walk through the valley of the shadow of death, I will fear no evil — *courage.*

For thou art with me; thy rod and thy staff they comfort me — *power.*

Thou preparest a table before me in the presence of mine enemies — *destiny.*

Thou anointest my head with oil — *wisdom.*

My cup runneth over — *understanding.*

Surely goodness and mercy shall follow me all the days of my life — *judgment.*

And I will dwell in the house of the Lord for ever — *fulfillment.*

Each morning, he jogs and utilizes this structure of the 23rd Psalm as the basis of prayer. Through this commitment, he is able to "let go and let God." Creative ideas flow from his spirit that produce productivity and profitability in his company. During this time of meditation on God's Word, the truly successful ideas for Dr. Lipke's business are born.

Prayer liberates us from the problems of the present with a vision of hope for the future. I have found that when we fail in prayer, we lose sight of who we are in Christ. We often start to focus on faults and limitations rather than redemption, renewal, and restoration. Through prayer, we find strength to overcome weaknesses within us and wisdom to solve problems around us.

The Lord Leads

The Cardone family attributes *all* of their success to creative ideas born of the leading of God's Spirit through prayer. Everyone has innate entrepreneurial tendencies, but truly creative entrepreneurs are those who recognize that "great ideas" come from God.

Michael Cardone, Jr. emphasized his father's strategy when he said, "This whole thing has evolved. We don't have a strategy of where we're going to be five years from now, but we keep praying and obeying. We are following the Lord. There does not really exist a 'five-year plan.' The Lord leads. If He brings us the people to help us manage (an aggressive five-year plan), then we'll build. If He doesn't, we don't do it."

One method they use to be certain their product remains a forerunner in the remanufactured automotive field is a twelve-month, 18,000-mile warranty. That their efforts are appreciated by their peers as well as by customers is shown by the fact that both father and son have been recognized and honored by the prestigious Automotive Hall of Fame and have twice been recipients of the coveted Automotive Service Industry Association's "Rebuilder of the Year" Award.

Principle Number Seven: Servant Leadership

11

Ruling From a Servant's Throne

American business and industry are suffering from a crisis of leadership. The crisis is two-fold: First, some of those in leadership have perverted their purpose and position. Second, many who should be leaders have failed to accept their responsibility. Both problems are related to the refusal of many people today to maintain self-discipline, or to rule over their own lives.

When I was young, one of the popular radio programs was "People Are Funny." On the show, participants were subjected to unfamiliar situations. We laughed at the reactions of those people, and their seeming stupidity. Yet we knew they really were no different than ourselves. We really were laughing at ourselves. So when we say that some people today have perverted their leadership roles and others have refused leadership, really we are pointing to ourselves.

Ruling One's Own Nature

I am sure this inability to rule one's own nature — which allows sin to rule in our natures to one degree or another — in modern Christians results from a lack of understanding of who God created man to be. Thus, we have low opinions of ourselves, or we overcompensate for those feelings and get into false confidence, which is pride. Real confidence and spiritual authority is based on a knowledge of God's

Word, His ways, and on maintaining spiritual authority over oneself.

Non-Christians do not have the knowledge of God nor the relationship it takes to walk in true leadership, and Christians look at their human weaknesses and forget the glorious truth that *we were created just a little lower than the angels* (Heb. 2:7).

Perhaps, too, the most disturbing truth about mankind is that we tend to insist on *having* a king rather than *being* kings. God's ultimate intention for us was that we were to be "servant-kings."

God gave man the mandate to subdue the Earth and rule over it, and His directive has not changed. Yet some of us seek to evade that predestined role and insist that someone, or something, else rule over us. We do not want responsibility. It is easier to let someone else tell us what to do. The simple truth is that by accepting God's purpose and accepting the role of servant-kings, we claim rulership over our own lives. To abdicate God's purpose is to abdicate the throne of our souls.

The prophet Daniel observed, **Hitherto is the end of the matter** (Dan. 7:28). He was referring to all that he had just written. What is the "matter" to which he was speaking with such finality and certainty? He stated it succinctly in Daniel 7:18:

> **But the saints of the most High shall take the kingdom, and possess the kingdom for ever, even for ever and ever.**

He restated this principle in Daniel 7:27:

> **And the kingdom and dominion, and the greatness of the kingdom under the whole heaven,**

**shall be given to the people of the saints of the most
High, whose kingdom is an everlasting kingdom, and
all dominions shall serve and obey him.**

This was truly a fantastic revelation, yet rather than
being excited, Daniel was troubled. Why? He was
troubled, I believe, because he knew human nature.
He knew they did not want to rule but would insist
on *having* kings rather than *being* kings, just as they had
in the early days of the nation of Israel when they had
demanded a king and Saul was set over them. (1 Sam.
8:6.) So Daniel kept the matter in his heart. (Dan. 7:28.)

Tyrants like Hitler arise because good men fail to
assume responsibility for ruling. Communism
continues to flourish, I believe, not because it is a good
system, but because people feel safer being controlled
rather than controlling.

The ultimate answer to fragmentation, division,
and Satan's insidious influence is for each person to
climb the ascendancy to his own throne. How is this
to be done?

Self-Discipline/Self-Control

The first step to climbing the throne in your own
life is *self-discipline and self-control.*

We can never have a throne in the world if we do
not rule our spirits to rule our souls (mind, will, and
emotions).

If we are to be leaders, we must first lead ourselves
properly. Jesus was offered the kingdoms of the world
by Satan, yet He knew the kingdoms really could not
be given away. Jesus' answer shows implicitly that the
issue was not the kingdoms but His own nature. He

understood He could never rightfully rule over others unless He first ruled over Himself. This was the key to Christ's strength. His spirit-man, the inner man, ruled His own soul and body, and thus He could accept rightful authority over others.

Society's Problems Caused by Lack of Self-Rule

Adam fell at this same point of testing. He wanted to *be as god* (Gen. 3:5), but yet refused to deny self or to control himself. God made the planet, then made man to rule, replenish, and fill the Planet Earth. God made the Garden for Adam and Eve, and the first couple had two jobs: to subdue the Earth and care for the Garden. The Garden was not to be isolated from the Earth, but rather was to be a model for what the Earth was to become through Adam's efforts. Adam's mandate was to extend the Garden throughout the entire Earth. His failure was that he chose to be ruled, or served, by the Garden, rather than exercising his rulership over the earth. The "Eden Syndrome" has been with mankind over since.

I have seen this same syndrome in the Church as it developed a monastic, self-serving view, turning inward rather than being a servant to the world. The Church became the new "Garden of Eden" when Christ came as "the last Adam." (1 Cor. 15:45.) Christians were the "Adams and Eves" of the New Covenant and were to extend the Garden (the Kingdom) into the world to serve the world. We were not told to retreat *from* the world, nor to be served *by* the world. We are called to minister, rather than be ministered unto.

Christ, the second and last Adam, walked out of the wilderness to become victorious over His own nature. He reclaimed for us the potential of making Daniel 7 a reality. For the first time since the Garden of Eden, Jesus returned the hope of self-rule, under God, to mankind.

The problems of our society have been caused by man not properly ruling himself. Man's greed is the result of inability to control lusts. The New Testament writer, James, described this by saying:

> But what about the feuds and struggles that exist among you — where do you suppose they come from? Can't you see that they arise from conflicting desires for pleasure within yourselves? You crave for something and don't get it; you are murderously jealous of what you can't possess yourselves; you struggle and fight with one another. You don't get what you want because you don't ask God for it. And when you do ask he doesn't give it to you, for you ask in quite the wrong spirit — you only want to satisfy your own desires.
>
> You are like unfaithful wives, never realising that to be the world's lover means becoming the enemy of God! Anyone who chooses to be the world's friend is thereby making himself God's enemy. Or do you think what the scriptures have to say about this is a mere formality? Do you imagine that this spirit of passionate jealousy is the Spirit he has caused to live in us? Yet he gives us grace which is stronger. That is why he says: God resisteth the proud, But giveth grace to the humble.
>
> Be humble then before God. But resist the devil and you'll find he'll run away from you. Come close to God and he will come close to you. You are sinners: get your hands clean again. Your loyalty is divided: get your hearts made true once more. You should be

deeply sorry, you should be grieved, you should even
be in tears. Your laughter will have to become
mourning, your high spirits will have to become
dejection. You must humble yourselves in the sight
of the Lord before he will lift you up.

James 4:1-10 JBP

God calls us to be kings on this earth. But we must
realize real and hard responsibilities come with this
calling. I am constantly drawn back to the days before
Israel had a king. God knew they would seek to be
ruled rather than to rule, so he covered this in
Deuteronomy 17. It is all about "reality for royalty."

Reality for Royalty

England's embattled Princess Margaret has been
embroiled in controversy most of her adult life. One
episode in the late Seventies resulted in a bitter battle
of words between the news media of both Canada and
the United States. The Canadian press began it by
criticizing England's decision to let the princess
represent Great Britain on a visit to Canada, citing her
"dubious" lifestyle as an objection.

Rising to the defense of their "persecuted"
princess, England's news media returned a vindictive
volley in two of its papers saying the Canadians live
in glass houses because they too had a "Maggie," who
was not exactly the epitome of staid British standards
of living. They suggested the Canadian attitude was
arrogant and judgmental. The maligned Princess
Margaret ended her tour and retreated to her home in
England, but that did not end the war of words.

Canada apparently had the last word, even though it might be considered somewhat bitter. An editorial in *The Toronto Star* "sassed" Mother England in this way:

> It is true that many countries have their embarrassments. We have our "Maggie" Trudeau. The United States had its Billy Carter, and England its Princess Margaret. However, only England is unwise enough to export its embarrassment.

Whether the war of words was undertaken "tongue in cheek" or taken seriously by some, the situation does point out that *royalty implies responsibility.* Kings are expected to act like kings, and their families are expected to live up to the standards worthy of high status. Jesus would agree with this principle. He said:

> . . . **For everyone to whom much is given, from him much will be required; and to whom much has been committed, of him they will ask the more.**
> **Luke 12:48 NKJV**

Kings Should Act Like Kings

A prominent engineer and Christian writer, the late Harold Hill, wrote a spate of books reminding believers of their unique status in being "King's kids." And he is right. We often live below our privileges. However, it also is urgent to remember a responsibility comes with royalty that demands more of us than the ordinary person. Paul wisely noted we are to:

> . . . **have a walk worthy of the calling with which you were called,**
>
> **with all lowliness and gentleness, with longsuffering, bearing with one another in love,**
>
> **endeavoring to keep the unity of the Spirit in the bond of peace.**
> **Ephesians 4:1-3 NKJV**

The responsibilities of royalty were solidly set down in Scripture long before Israel ever had a king. This should not be a surprise because Amos noted: **Surely the Lord God does nothing, unless He reveals His secret to His servants the prophets** (Amos 3:7 NKJV).

And those responsibilities of royalty carry over to our time since John says: **To Him who loved us and washed us from our sins in His own blood, and has made us kings and priests to His God and Father . . .** (Rev. 1:5,6 NKJV).

Thus, it is not enough that we enjoy the privilege of being a "King's kid," we must also understand our relating responsibilities. There are four of these outlined in Deuteronomy 17:16-20, and at first reading, they seem strange to us because the principles are expressed in terms of the culture of that day. But careful consideration of them speaks volumes to us today on how we are to act and react in our homes and on our jobs.

The first three had to do with piling up possessions. They admonished a king not to make himself rich at the expense of the people whom he was supposed to serve.

He Shall Not Multiply Horses, Wives, Nor Silver and Gold

Horses were used exclusively in Old Testament days as animals of war. Only once in the Bible is there an allusion of horses being utilized for any other reason than destruction (Is. 28:28) or perhaps idolatry (2 Kings 23:11). When Jesus rode into Jerusalem on a donkey, it was by design as well as for fulfillment of prophecy. He wanted to express Himself as the "Prince of Peace," not as a prince of war. Thus, he chose an animal of peace, not an animal of war. God wanted the kings of Israel to be men of peace, not of conflict, but tragically, all of the kings disregarded and discarded this key commandment to the coming kings of Israel.

David set the pace in multiplying horses. He established a force of cavalry and chariots (2 Sam. 8:4), but his famous son brought disobedience of this commandment to its ultimate. Solomon was very active in the horse-trading business, having horses brought out of Egypt and resold to the Hittites.

This rich and famous king owned thousands of horses and even established "chariot cities," such as Megiddo, which guarded a pass on the high road (the "King's Road") from Syria to Egypt. In these cities, Solomon had stalls constructed with cobbled floors in order to keep unshod hooves from slipping. These stables of the king housed at least four hundred and fifty horses each. A chariot "team" was made up of three horses, two in harness and one in reserve.

Solomon did all of this in spite of the distinct warning:

> **"But he shall not multiply horses for himself, nor cause the people to return to Egypt to multiply horses, for the Lord has said to you, 'You shall not return that way again.' "**
>
> **Deuteronomy 17:16 NKJV**

Solomon also, as most Christians are aware from reading the Bible, multiplied wives — considered a sign

173

of wealth in those days — and also laid up silver and gold at the expense of the people.

He Shall Write for Himself a Copy of This Law

The fourth commandment for kings found in Deuteronomy 17 was for each king to write out a copy of the entire law from the scroll possessed by the priests. This probably meant for him to write out in his own hand, for his own benefit, the book of Deuteronomy.

Psychologists have learned that most of our problems are internal rather than external. While circumstances may create discomfort, it is our reaction to them that determines our feelings and ability to function. This is best articulated in an old familiar poem:

"Two men look out through the same bars. One sees the mud, and one the stars."[1]

Circumstances may be similar for many people, but their reactions are determined by what is inside them. That is why this commandment was given for the guidance of Israel's future kings, and why it still has much meaning for us today.

The reason this fourth directive makes so much sense today is that it is often easy to *act* like a Christian but far more difficult to *react* like one.

Some of us live our religious lives like a swimmer who attempts to keep a beach ball under water. As long

---

[1]Frederick Langbridge, "Pessimist and Optimist," *Sound and Sense: An Introduction to Poetry,* ed. Laurence Perrine (New York: Harcourt Brace Jovanovich, 1977), p. 100.

as he keeps his hand on the ball and pays close attention, he can keep the globe beneath the waves. But the minute his attention is diverted, the ball pops up to the surface again.

So it is with those who have a surface relationship with Christ. As long as they pay close attention to their actions, they can do all the right things to impress others and themselves with their own righteousness. But when "push comes to shove," it is a different story. The ball bursts out of the water and reveals us for what we are.

It is simply true that all of us are nice people until someone messes with us. Then it becomes painfully obvious to everyone around us who is ruling us: the Holy Spirit or our own souls.

By writing out the Word rather than just having it read to him, the new king of Israel would begin to *internalize* God's principles for the kingdom. However, it was not to be a one-time experience like reading a novel or even reading the constitution of a nation. Rather, it was for a long-term purpose.

> **"And it shall be with him, and he shall read it all the days of his life, that he may learn to fear the Lord his God and be careful to observe all the words of this law and these statutes."**
> **Deuteronomy 17:19 NKJV**

God's Priority Is Relationships

Just as God wanted His Israelite kings to be men of peace, the New Covenant reminds us of His priority for us:

> **And a servant of the Lord must not quarrel but be gentle to all, able to teach, patient,**

in humility correcting those who are in opposition, if God will perhaps grant them repentance, so that they may know the truth.

2 Timothy 2:24,25 NKJV

The Bible is a book of relationships and the devil's aim from the beginning has been to interrupt relationships. Ever since Adam sinned, man has been at war with God, and ever since Cain murdered Abel, we have been at war with one another. Jesus reduced the entire Bible to twenty-nine words:

. . . love the Lord your God with all your heart, with all your soul, with all your mind, and with all your strength.

. . . You shall love your neighbor as yourself.
Mark 12:30,31 NKJV

Paul, who had been cut by the sharp edges of broken relationships and had himself hurt others, made a passionate plea to the church at Ephesus:

And do not grieve the Holy Spirit of God, by whom you were sealed for the day of redemption.
Ephesians 4:30 NKJV

Paul wrote this admonition in the context of relationships and those things that contribute to a breakdown in fellowship. In Ephesians, he discussed truthfulness, self-control, dealing properly with anger, honesty, hard work, kindness in communication, forgiveness, understanding, and tenderheartedness as all necessary ingredients to build and retain relationships. He then cautioned that we bring grief to the Holy Spirit when we refuse to work through relationships and to cooperate with the plan of God. That plan is to reconcile man to God and man to his brother.

Relationships always have priority in Scripture. Jesus told us clearly how to work through difficult relationships when we are hurt by someone else in Matthew 18:21-35. He even linked our forgiveness from God to our forgiveness toward those who hurt us.

Peter frankly says interrupted relationships with others interrupts our relationship with God:

> **Likewise you husbands, dwell with them with understanding, giving honor to the wife, as to the weaker vessel, and as being heirs together of the grace of life, that your prayers may not be hindered.**
>
> **1 Peter 3:7** NKJV

We are to be people of peace, not of conflict:

> **For he who would love life and see good days, Let him refrain his tongue from evil, And his lips from speaking guile:**
>
> **Let him turn away from evil and do good; Let him seek peace and pursue it.**
>
> **1 Peter 3:10,11** NKJV

Our Problems Are Internal

When the well-known Christian leader Tim LaHaye chose to challenge the Humanists at their 1981 convention in San Diego, the debate heated up and tempers flared. Speaking for the American Humanist Association, Dr. Gerald Larue said to LaHaye:

> Where we would differ with you, sir, is that we would deny the right of people who have been dead for two thousand to three thousand years to control and condition our time and our state and our thinking. We are not where they were, they are not where we are.[2]

---

[2]Frederick Edwords, "The LaHaye-Larue Dialogue," *Humanist Magazine*, July-Aug. 1981, p. 14.

Perhaps the eminent doctor merely was incensed by LaHaye's argument and spoke rashly. However, if Larue really feels the way he stated, he certainly seems to be shortsighted and even extremely naive. If we ignore collected wisdom from our history, we are foolish people. And if that wisdom is revelation, then the problem is even more acute. Obviously, Dr. Larue does not see the Bible as revelation. However, ignoring history from even a secular viewpoint is unwise.

It should be remembered that the way men approach their problems today is not really different from how they have always dealt with them. And if it is true most of our problems are internal rather than external, then obviously the collected wisdom of the ages cannot be shut off like a hydrant. If it is shut off, then each new generation must relearn all the lessons of the past. Such shortsightedness would doom mankind to a primitive cave man existence forever. In addition, if one believes Jesus is really alive, then His principles certainly are applicable for today's bewildering world.

God told the kings to take advantage of the wisdom of the past and not be forced to reinvent the wheel. He told them to pay attention to the principles of the law laid down, and good would come to them. Centuries later, the Apostle Paul would underline that argument by speaking of Old Testament annals in this way:

> **Now all these things happened to them as examples, and they are written for our admonition, on whom the ends of the ages have come.**
>
> **1 Corinthians 10:11 NKJV**

Promises and Commandments Have Purposes

Promises have purpose and so do commandments. Moses concludes his kingly admonitions by noting the benefits to the kings who would listen. He said:

> . . .**be careful to observe all the words of this law and these statutes,**
>
> **That his heart may not be lifted above his brethren, that he may not turn aside from the commandment to the right hand or to the left, and that he may prolong his days in his kingdom, he and his children in the midst of Israel.**
>
> **Deuteronomy 17:19,20 NKJV**

The Bible is not merely a "cry for justice," "a cry for kindness," or a "Golden Rule." Rather, it is the revealed Word and will of God. It is the "Owner's Manual" for believers, and if followed, it will insure that we end up where He wants. If the Word is ignored, we bounce against the walls of our lives and bruise ourselves deeply. Without doubt there is responsibility in being a King's kid. But with this responsibility comes all the rights of royalty that so many Christian writers are explaining.

Perhaps it would be well to remember that it is the *way of the transgressor* that is hard, not the *way of the believer*. A believer should not have to worry about gambling debts, or sweat over the bank or his company discovering his embezzlement, or the tax man discovering "hanky-panky." He should not be worrying about his mistress calling his wife.

No wonder the Bible says:

> **For this is the love of God, that we keep His
> commandments. And His commandments are not
> burdensome.**
>
> **1 John 5:3** NKJV

When the kings of Israel learned that God's ways were best and practiced them, they were blessed. Tragically, most of them never lived up to the knowledge they had. Thus the lineage of kings of Israel and Judah is drawn in blood. Hopefully, we modern "kings and priests unto God" need not make the same mistakes. Like the law of gravity, the moral laws of our universe have not changed and the unchanging God still speaks in the same language in which He has always spoken. Fortunately we can listen, learn, and live responsibly as twentieth century royalty. As *the* King's kids, we also can act like it.

There are several truths we should keep in mind concerning what God expects of us.

Three Truths:
Purpose, Choice, and Consequence

The first truth is that God has a purpose for everyone. No one is exempt. His overall purpose is for each of His children to become a servant-king. To each one, He gives a specific area where that individual can work out the application of God's overall purpose.

The second truth is that we may accept or reject God's specific purpose in our lives. God will not force anything upon anyone. This is the reality of free will. We must choose, but we win or lose by the way we choose.

The third truth is that there is a consequence that follows our choices. If we accept God's purpose and seek to work out His will in our lives, we will benefit and prosper as He has promised. However, if we reject our purpose and position, our refusal yields negative consequences for ourselves and for those around us.

I am reminded of this third truth when I read Judges 8:22-35. Gideon had led his country for many years. He had been chosen, ordained, and called of God. As a successful leader, he was approached by the people of Israel to rule and to establish a line of rulers so they would be assured of a ruler in the future. Israel needed leadership. They had seen God's miracles and were looking for a man of God to lead them. Gideon had set an example to which they could aspire. They needed a leader like him to show them maturity and prosperity. Note what Gideon did.

At first, we are impressed with his response, "I won't lead you, but God will lead you."

He put up a very spiritual facade, using wonderful religious rhetoric. But there was something wrong. God rules, blesses, and works through people.

What Gideon was really saying was, "Thanks but no thanks. I don't want the responsibility. God can rule over you without me."

While his rejection was bad enough, Gideon went farther. Rather than choosing to serve his people, he built a monument for the people to serve. He refused responsibility, and that led to idolatry. He brought destruction to his people and to himself.

Gideon made three mistakes. First, he made friendship with the world. This is found in Judges 8:31 where his affair with a concubine is related. The son born of that relationship, Abimelech, would use bribes and murder to gain the throne his father had refused. (Judg. 9.)

Gideon's second mistake was rejecting God by rejecting God's purpose.

His third mistake was to build a monument to himself. In spite of the fact that Gideon was a godly man, he made these three tragic mistakes, and his family and nation paid dearly for generations.

Things held together rather well until Gideon died. Then the nation was in turmoil, having fallen completely into idolatry. Abimelech killed all but one of Gideon's legitimate sons. He slaughtered seventy of them on the same execution block. (Judg. 9:5.) Only Jotham was left alive. He went up to the top of Mount Gerizim and called out to the men of Shechem. Then he told them a parable about an olive tree, a fig tree, and a vine. (Judg. 9:7-15.)

The trees one day decided to choose a ruler. First they approached the olive tree to rule over them. The olive produced oil used for healing as well as for food. Oil soothes, calms, and promotes healing of wounds. The olive tree is used in Scripture as a symbol of peace, unity, and healing. But that God-intended leadership failed to respond responsibly.

Next, the fig tree was approached. Figs are sweet fruit, and sweetness symbolically represents the right relationships. But again this God-intended purpose was thwarted by refusal to respond to responsibility.

Finally, the vine was approached. From the vine comes grapes which produce wine. Wine is a symbol for happiness and joy. But again, the vine refused to respond. In Jotham's parable, the people approach potential rulers who exhibit the attributes of godly kings. Yet all the good men refused. That set the stage for evil to rise.

Note the result of the abdication of the good men: a "bramblebush king" grew up to fill the void.

Evil comes in where righteous men fail. If we fail to rule ourselves, we will be ruled by sin. If we fail to rule our children, they will be ruled by sin. If we fail to rule in our churches, they will be ruled by division and sin. If we fail to rule our nation, it will be ruled by destruction and sin.

We Must Not Abdicate Leadership

God rules through men. Without righteous men to exercise God's rule over the world, what alternative is life? If you and I and our neighbors abdicate our thrones of servant-leadership, what will happen? None will rise up to take our place in righteousness, but there will come "bramblebush kings" to fill the void. Decay, dissolution, and destruction set in. Fire comes out of the bramble and devours the cedars of Lebanon.

God has work for each of us that no one else can do. There is a song only we can sing, a love only we can give, a word only we can say. If we fail to accept our responsibility of servant-leadership, ruling over ourselves, our families, our jobs, and in our communities, there will come a "bramblebush king," who brings destruction.

Abraham Lincoln wisely said, "We get the kind of leadership we deserve."

Dr. Lipke and both Cardones, senior and junior, have accepted their responsibilities. I see others like them doing the same thing. Through this responsible leadership, God can bring peace, productivity, and prosperity. My deepest prayer is that all of us recognize our responsibility and move into our work sites to return the kingdom to our Father.

Let us reclaim the country! We can, and I believe we will!

Principle Number Eight:
Spiritual Renewal

12

A Spiritual Stirring: A Crisis of Spirit

The crisis in American capitalism is fundamentally a crisis of spirit, requiring a moral solution rather than a simple economic one.[1]
— *The Deindustrialization of America*

The problems faced by our nation, so evident in western New York and other steel communities, are not new. America has faced similar troubles before. Back in the 1800s, Rochester, New York, was a thriving grain-mill town. The mills were the heart of the community's economy which supported a diversity of other family-owned and -operated businesses.

Farmers brought their grain to town where they sold it to the mills and purchased goods from merchants. Skilled craftsmen, who turned out everything from shoes to furniture, were numerous. More than half the adult male population labored at specialized skills in family businesses.

As the years passed and the community prospered, the situation began to change. The success of the community drew a massive influx of new people. At one time, it was estimated that one hundred and twenty men left Rochester each day, while one hundred

---

[1]Bluestone and Harrison, *The Deindustrialization of America* (New York: Basic Books, 1982) p. 13.

and thirty more arrived. To bring control into the chaos, business owners began to apply tighter controls over the labor force. Close-knit family businesses employed a few outside workers, who many times, boarded at the homes of their employers.

Then the system began to unravel. As the population grew and "boom times" arrived, businesses were forced to expand to meet demand. This expansion meant a larger work force, a dilution of traditional skills, narrower specialization of skills, and an increasing distance between labor and management.

Paul E. Johnson describes the situation in his book, *A Shopkeeper's Millenium:*

> Masters increased the pace, scale, and regularity of production, and they hired young strangers with whom they shared no more than contractual obligations. The masters were becoming businessmen, concerned more with the purchase of labor and raw materials and the distribution of finished goods than with the production itself.

> They began to absent themselves from the workshops. At the same time, they demanded new standards of discipline and regularity within those rooms.[2]

Not only did the shopkeepers begin to distance themselves from their shops, they became increasingly disinterested in the lives of their workers outside of work. When skilled laborers lived with or next door to a master craftsman or shop owner, they shared their

---

[2]Paul E. Johnson, *A Shopkeeper's Millenium* (New York: Hill and Wang, 1978), p. 57.

lives as well as their work. Now workers lived in distant neighborhoods, separated by new class barriers.

The situation resulted in increased disruption of society and its morality. Drinking and drunkenness among workers became a serious problem, accompanied by violence. Politics suffered also as men with wealth began to abuse their power through bribery and intimidation. Bitter political rivalries often extended into the churches, and factions sought to control the various congregations. Soon the situation in Rochester was one of near hopelessness.

Johnson writes:

By the end of the decade, churchgoing businessmen and masters had lost faith in their ability to govern. Beneath them was a new and unruly and altogether necessary urban working class. Masters had always governed such men spontaneously, in face-to-face transactions that were a part of everyday routine. That system collapsed in the middle and late 1820s. Now attempts to influence the actions of working men through authority and persuasion were unsuccessful and worse — humiliating. Village officials, elected by the majority that many wished to regulate, did nothing.

In 1828, some militant Christian businessmen tried to re-establish control through force. They failed, and in the course of failing, they split the church-going community into warring camps. By 1830, the temperance and Sabbatarian crusades were bankrupt and ready to dissolve, and mystified church members fought each other until they were numb.

The life went out of Rochester Protestantism. After steady gains throughout the 1820s, and a hopeful revival in 1827, conversions stopped. In every church,

the number of new members dropped dramatically in
1828 and 1829 and through the fall of 1830.[3]

Parallels in the Twentieth Century

I see some modern parallels. The similarities
between the plight of business and industry then and
now seem to be obvious. There is a crisis in Christian
leadership. As then, today I see some Christians
speaking out on the problems, but their analyses of the
situation does not seem to offer real hope. The Church
has accepted the word of the secular economists, who
have announced the death of industry and the rise of
an information-based society.

Next, I see some religious leaders attempting to
bring change through force. Rather than seeking
reconciliation, they have opted for dramatic and often
violent confrontation. While I understand the
frustration, I believe such action is doomed to failure.
The problems are too complex for force to be effective.
It is not a matter of chasing money changers from the
temple, and it is not a time for confrontation and
hostility. Violence can only be counterproductive, with
bad feelings and broken bodies.

The Church already is divided over how to solve
the problems of our society. To me, this is the most
serious problem. Disunity in the Body disrupts the flow
of God's power, and if we cannot solve our own
disagreements, how can we help others? The Bible calls
us to be "likeminded" and "of one mind." God's
expressed desire for the Church is to come into a unity

---

[3]Ibid., p. 93.

of faith. This does not mean we all must join the same denomination. Rather, it means simply that we recognize our relationship to each other, based on our relationship to God. We are God's children; therefore, we are all brothers and sisters in faith. Through a unity of faith will come renewal, revival, and restoration.

The Power of Prayer To Change Things

I see hope in what happened in Rochester. Back in 1829, one of the elders of a church in the area wrote to a well-known evangelist — Charles Finney. The historian records:

> He (the elder) confessed that the good people of Rochester felt powerless to do anything about it:
>
> "The people and the church say it cannot be helped — and why do they say this? Because the state of religion is so low; because they know not the power of the Gospel of Jesus. Through Christ Jesus strengthening us we can do all things, and if so it is time we were about it." After describing the situation, the elder invited Finney to Rochester for a revival.
>
> Charles Grandison Finney came to Rochester in September, 1930. For six months he preached in Presbyterian churches nearly every night and three times on Sunday, and his audience included members of every sect. During the day he prayed with individuals and led an almost continuous series of prayer meetings. Soon there were simultaneous meetings in churches and homes throughout the village. Pious women went door-to-door praying for troubled souls. The high school stopped classes and prayed. Businessmen closed their doors early and prayed with their families. "You could not go upon the streets," recalled one convert, "and hear any conversation except upon religion."

By early spring the churches faced the world with a militance and unity that had been unthinkable only months before, and with a boundless and urgent sense of their ability to change society. In the words of its closest student, "No more impressive revival has occurred in American history."[4]

There are two crucial elements to Finney's revival. First, the power of prayer was overwhelming. Historians say nearly everyone was involved in ongoing, fervent prayer. Then evangelism flowed out of the churches into the community and workplace. Johnson states later, "The revival made an evangelist of every convert . . . ."[5]

Following the revival, the churches filled with new members, businessmen began caring again for their workers, and alcoholism dropped dramatically, as did the violence and corruption. The community was restored to dignity, productivity, and unity. Johnson says the real birth of America's middle class came as a *direct result* of the Finney revival.

Another factor in Finney's revival was that massive personal evangelism followed. Prayer transferred to power to change the community. We must infiltrate God's dream into society, one person at a time. Jesus called us "fishers of men." (Matt. 4:19.)

Modern Day "Evangelists" in the Marketplace

In today's business world, M. Cardone Industries has openly advanced the cause of Christ since its

---

[4]Ibid., p. 94,95.

[5]Ibid., p. 95.

inception. Both father and son are deeply spiritual men, as are their plant leaders, or officers. Michael Cardone, Sr. has seen his company, started as a result of prayer, become a materialization of his dreams.

Started on his 55th birthday in 1970, he says, "God has allowed me to realize my dream of having a company that puts Him first in every decision."

Nor is his dream restricted to his own company. He is a founding regent of Oral Roberts University in Tulsa, Oklahoma. The university has awarded him an honorary doctorate for his leadership and contributions. Many other religious institutions have benefited from his priority of putting God first in all things. This has been reflected, also, in his promotion and support of the three ethnic churches initiated in his main plant but which now have their own facilities.

Michael Cardone, Jr. says, "Our purpose as a business is to make a profit. One of our objectives is to evangelize, but it is not the reason for our existence."

This desire to evangelize is evident in the daily chapels, Bible fellowships, appointment of resident chaplains, and youth programs, all with religious emphases. Employees also are invited to attend church on Sundays.

Cardone's dealings with business contacts reflect the same concern. Michael Jr. says, "Show a business-man how he can make money with your product, and you have his attention. Giving him a good product and delivering it when he wants it is going to communicate to him more than preaching will. Then all of a sudden he comes back and says, 'What is it with you guys?

How do you operate? What is it with your company?'
Then we can share the love of Christ. But only if you
show them something first. They have to see the love
of Jesus in operation before they want to hear about it."

Renewal and Servant-Leadership

We are called to catch men for the kingdom, to
launch out into the deep (the world) and catch men
for Christ. Note Jesus did not say just to "go fish" for
men. It is not taking a pole down to the lazy river,
propping it up on a rock, and then lying back and
taking a nap waiting for a "nibble." Rather, Jesus said,
"Thou *shalt* catch men. You *will* do it! You will go out,
with the net of my Word, and you will catch men." This
is not a passive attitude. It is a call to action. We must
respond.

Becoming fishers of men rather than fishers of fish
reflects the idea of servanthood. While Peter was fishing
for fish, he was concerned primarily with meeting his
own needs. The same is true when we work for money.
However, when we take the focus of our efforts off the
fish and put it on to fishing for men, we become a
source of provision for others.

God calls us to become fishers of men, to turn our
focus on serving rather than on being served. This is
the crux of success. We are called to be successful in
our own lives through helping others succeed in their
lives. This is the Jesus Principle, summed up by John:

> This is my commandment, That ye love one
> another, as I have loved you.
>
> Greater love hath no man than this, that a man
> lay down his life for his friends.
>
> John 15:12,13

Servant-leaders demand excellence from workers, and demanding excellence from others means one must first demand excellence of oneself.

Dr. Lipke says, "I am demanding of others, but I'm more demanding of myself. The higher a person is in the company, the harder I am on him. When I make a mistake, I take the blame for it all they way. When a division president messes up, I get pretty steamed, and he knows about it. But if a cleaning person makes a mistake, I am almost pleasant as I reprimand him. I understand the levels of responsibility."

A servant-leader in industry and business seeks to serve others more than self and creates an image employees can respect and trust.

Dr. Lipke says, "A person may do business with me and not like my personality, clothes, or the style in which I conduct the business meeting. But he has to admit my openness. I have made honesty my hallmark. At Gibraltar, our word is our bond, and we stand behind it, no matter what it costs us. At times one of my people has made a promise that normally we really couldn't keep. But I will go outside our area of expertise and buy material in order for us to meet that commitment. That is why we are named *Gibraltar*, just like the rock. We are rock solid on our word.

"In fact, we often go beyond the commitment of our promise and do more than is expected. We have experienced blessings because we were bold enough to put our customers' needs before our own welfare."

Renewal can come in American business and industry. But it will come only if each of us begins to live out God's principles in the workplace. And we can begin where we are, as janitor, secretary, salesman, clerk, accountant, computer programmer, manager, owner, or whatever our position. The renewal in the Church or in industry must start in the hearts of men. We must reach out with the net of God's Word, with love and concern, and start catching men for the Kingdom.

Through prayer, God brings into alignment the motives of our hearts and spirits with the higher purposes of His heart and Spirit. Through prayer, He gives us the vision, the dream, the ideas that can transform our world.

As we respond to His dreams and visions, we can put His Word into action and touch the lives of others. Just as Finney's revival swept through Rochester and affected all of North America, we can see renewal in our own lifetime. Renewal and revival will come, and you can be a part of it. You *must* be a part of it! As the revival and renewal come, we will see the results in our attitudes and actions. I have found that our attitudes and actions often have been molded by our environment rather than what God wants of us. As renewal occurs, I believe it will start affecting how we treat one another and how we live out our respect for each other on the work site. Lately, I have been haunted by how we treat one another in our speech.

13

Famous Last Words: Speech Has Power

"If I'm a legend, then why am I so lonely?" were among the last words of famed entertainer Judy Garland, before she died of a drug overdose on June 22, 1969.[1]

Not nearly so despairing were the words of inventor Thomas Edison, who apparently had made his peace with God. He breathed his last saying, "It's very beautiful over there."[2]

O. Henry (William Sidney Porter), the writer of classic short stories, gasped, "Turn up the lights. I don't want to go home in the dark."[3]

Some questioned the spiritual status of writer-philosopher Henry David Thoreau as he lay dying in 1862. His Aunt Louisa asked if he had made his peace with God.

Thoreau's reply was, "I did not know we had ever quarreled, Aunt."[4]

---

[1]Norman and Betty Donaldson, *How Did They Die?* (New York: St. Martin's Press, 1980), p. 127.

[2]Ibid., p. 107.

[3]Ibid., p. 169.

[4]Ibid., p. 362.

When another friend visited the dying man and told him of a spring robin, he said, "Yes, this is a beautiful world; but I shall see a fairer."[5]

William Somerset Maugham was not so assured as he labored his last breaths. Shortly before he died in 1965, the world-renowned author told his nephew, Robin Maugham, "I've been a horrible and evil man. Every single one of the few people who have ever got to know me well has ended up by hating me."[6]

Then the last words he whispered to his nephew were, "If you believe in prayer, then pray that I won't wake up in the morning."[7]

Last words long have been accepted for their truth and as a barometer of the soul about to set off for the journey into eternity. This prompted William Shakespeare to note:

> O, but they say the tongues of dying men enforce attention like deep harmony: Where words are scarce, they are seldom spent in vain, For they breath truth that breath their words in pain.[8]

The Last Words of Jesus

Understanding the importance of last words, perhaps it would be wise to consider the last words of our Lord and three of those who lived closest to Him. In doing so, we learn an urgent pattern of speech that

---

[5]Ibid., p. 361.

[6]Ibid., p. 254.

[7]Ibid.

[8]William Shakespeare, *King Richard II*, Act II, Scene I.

should be part of our daily conversation and not merely the dribble from our dying lips.

Each of the writers of the gospels records his own version of the last words of our Lord, and Luke does so twice, by writing the book of Acts. Although the words differ in arrangement, they have the same content. Therefore, it would be well to select the last words of Jesus as recorded in the first gospel. Matthew notes that Jesus said three things before He ascended to the Father.

First, he reminded His followers of His power: **All power is given unto me in heaven and in earth** (Matt. 28:18). This had an impact because the disciples knew as long as he lived in them, there was nothing in this world or the world to come that could conquer them. They were given His authority.

Then Jesus commissioned them by saying they were not only to snatch souls from the burning, but also to teach all nations, and to baptize His followers. This meant that those who would follow after the Master must be totally identified with Him in keeping His commandments and in dedication to His service.

Finally, Jesus said, **Lo, I am with you alway, even unto the end of the world** (Matt. 28:20).

There would be no circumstance facing them that would separate His presence from them. He was their "portable God."

In other words, they were the Temple of the Holy Spirit, and that meant wherever they went, He went. It was a mind-expanding idea. No longer must worshipers go to a temple to get in contact with God.

Rather, now He would live forever in them in their success or in their sorrow. The apostles grasped this concept and forever preached it in such magnificent chapters as Romans 8 and Hebrews 13.

The last words of our Lord were words of *assurance.*

The Last Words of John

John was identified as the "disciple Jesus loved." Obviously He loved them all, but there was something special about John. He had learned to listen to and lean on Jesus. He developed from a brash and somewhat harsh youth to the apostle of love. He had learned a lot along the way, and the Holy Spirit used him to pen five books of the New Testament.

His last words probably were written later. Still, Third John is his own words written under the inspiration of the Holy Spirit, not just a narrative of the One he loved most or a recording of the words of His Master. As an old man, John wrote to a dear friend named Gaius. His letter is one of commendation and care.

John expressed his holy desire for his friend and praised him for his generous attitudes toward traveling ministers. (3 John 2-8.) Then the apostle took a moment to warn about a selfish man, Diotrephes, and his egocentric activities. (vv. 9-11.) John was careful to give full credit to another who has a good report of all men. (v. 12.) He told his friend how he longed for fellowship with him and took care to instruct Gaius to **Greet the friends by name** (vv. 13-15).

John wanted to be sure all those dear brothers and sisters in Christ knew just how important they were to him and how grateful he was that God had inter-twined his life with theirs in friendship. Perhaps the most poignant of John's last words are: **I have no greater joy than to hear that my children walk in truth** (3 John 4).

John's last words are those of *approval*.

The Last Words of Paul

Paul, born as he described, "out of due time" (1 Cor. 15:8), still impacted his world, although he got a later start as an apostle. Many of the New Testament books carry his signature. Fulfillment of Christ's command to reach the uttermost parts of the earth largely were carried out by this brilliant, aggressive, and determined man who drove himself beyond endurance to be identified with our Lord.

Now old and about to be beheaded, Paul wrote his spiritual "last will and testament" from a Roman prison to a young son in the faith. His second pastoral epistle to Timothy is far more than that. It is a personal statement that all was well with his soul even after beatings, abuses, shipwrecks, imprisonments, and rejections. One can hardly read the last words of Paul without feeling a surge of joy and faith because his last words were filled with faith.

Paul talked about a good finish, saying he had completed the assignment the Master teacher had given him, and it was ready to be turned in personally by him. He ventured a comment that it was a good finish, and little room was left for regrets. (2 Tim. 4:6-7.)

Then he moved on to talk of a good future. This seems even stranger, considering the backdrop of the cold, damp prison and the threat of the executioner's sword. Yet Paul wrote:

> **Henceforth there is laid up for me a crown of righteousness, which the Lord, the righteous judge, shall give me at that day: and not to me only, but unto all them also that love his appearing.**
>
> **2 Timothy 4:8**

Finally, he wrote about good friends. (vv. 19-22.) True, some had failed Paul, but the list of those who stood by him was far greater, and he wanted the world to know he loved and appreciated them.

In a great burst of faith, Paul cried in the middle of these tributes:

> **And the Lord shall deliver me from every evil work, and will preserve me unto his heavenly kingdom: to whom be glory forever and ever. Amen.**
>
> **2 Timothy 4:18**

The sword might sever his head from his body, but the spirit would be delivered to God intact, and Paul knew a glorious place awaited him.

Paul's last words were those of *anticipation*.

The Last Words of Peter

Peter always had something to say about almost everything, and he certainly left us powerful and positive last words to think about. Second Peter records these from his lips, and they center on how to live, how to love, and how to leave. Peter said all of us need to live in glorious expectation of the coming of Christ, looking for that new world that will come with the Lord's appearance. (2 Pet. 3:11-13.)

He then moved quickly on to tell his friends to keep their heads in the clouds but their feet firmly planted on the earth. He said that we are to live in peace and to hold firm to the glorious gospel of Christ that has been delivered to us. Then he encouraged them — and us:

> But grow in grace, and in the knowledge of our Lord and Saviour Jesus Christ. To Him be glory both now and for ever. Amen.
>
> 2 Peter 3:18

If we isolate the most poignant of Peter's last words, they would have to be these:

> The Lord is not slack concerning his promise, as some men count slackness; but is longsuffering to us-ward, not willing that any should perish, but that all should come to repentance.
>
> 2 Peter 3:9

Peter sums up his whole wild and bumpy ride to the Father by showing deepest appreciation for God's promises, His patience (How Peter needed that!), and His persistent love for the lost.

Peter's last words were those of *appreciation.*

In reviewing the last words of those four, a clear pattern emerges. Their speech centers on assurance, approval, anticipation, and appreciation. Of the many last things they could have said, they chose these because of their importance.

Perhaps it would be well to ask, "What were the last words I spoke to my mate, my children, my employer, my employees, my neighbor?"

Were they words of assurance, approval, anticipation, and appreciation, or were they words such as the rest of the world speaks? The language of this earth is foreign to that which the true follower of Christ speaks.

The Accent of Our "Native" Land

Even a casual observation of the speech patterns of this world sees curses, criticism, doubt, and selfishness being spoken. It is evil that makes the headlines and obscenity that bloats the speeches of mortal man. Despair and destruction fill out our songs; hatred and anger flesh out our speeches. Negativism and fear of ultimate atomic destruction form the verbal backdrop of our lives.

Yet God's children have been given a new language. The heavenly language is one that only the children of the Kingdom can speak. It is not the language of the streets but the language of hope.

Read again the prophets and the apostles. While they deal with severe and deep problems in their societies, the overall tone of their words is that of assurance, approval, anticipation, and appreciation. The prophets and apostles all spoke the same language because they came from the same country. Just as an earthly dialect identifies the speaker, so the tone of our conversation betrays our spiritual citizenship.

Followers of Jesus can and must live as victors, not as victims. We have different principles, powers, and resources. But how will the world know unless we begin to talk this "heavenly language" of faith? Our conversation and mindset are different because we are born from above and have our citizenship in another country. Thus, our speech should reflect the accent of our native land.

Like God, we can speak worlds into existence. If we reflect the gloom, despair, and tensions of this life in our speech, we have spoken such a world into existence. If we speak hostility, we create a world that is cold and hard around us. We carry that world wherever we go. On the other hand, by speaking in that "other tongue" — the language of Heaven, which is the language of faith, hope, and love — we speak that world into being. And we must live in whatever world we create.

May we begin speaking words of assurance, approval, anticipation, and appreciation in our homes, work sites, neighborhoods, churches, and the world at large. Our last words in any conversation should reflect one or all of these qualities. Peter reminds us:

> **But ye are a chosen generation, a royal priesthood, an holy nation, a peculiar people; that ye should shew forth the praises of him who hath called you out of darkness into his marvellous light.**
> **1 Peter 2:9**

A final note is mandatory. God called the ten spies' report "evil." (Num. 14:37.) He did not say the report was *false*. They had accurately described the natural conditions of the Promised Land. There *were* giants there, and the prospect to take the land *did* look dim. The report was accurate, *but evil because it was not based on faith.* Left alone, Israel certainly could not have conquered the land. However, God never intended them to do it alone. He was to be their predominant partner in the taking process.

Without doubt, there are overwhelming odds against us in this world. There are many reasons why we cannot succeed — but all of them leave out God. With Him we are a majority. Therefore, the words of assurance, approval, anticipation, and appreciation are not hyped-up positive mental attitudes. Rather, they flow from a heart that sees things not as they are, but what they will become through our partnership with Him.

Each Challenge Is Personal

My thoughts went back again to that day I traversed the Father Baker Bridge, and the Lord spoke to me, asking, "Could you speak to these dry bones, and make them live again?"

More succinctly than ever, I realized the power of words, and how they mold the world. Only through speaking in faith can we hope to effect a better world in which to live. Spiritual renewal within a community will inevitably change men's hearts. Changed hearts will produce changed conversation.

I submit not only our need for a spiritual renewal, but that this impending spiritual renewal will enable us to speak creative words to our society. Words of assurance and anticipation to our business community. Employer will be enabled to speak words of approval to his employee. And employee will be able to speak words of appreciation to his employer.

And with that we come to an urgent text for life:

Let the words of my mouth, and the meditation of my heart, be acceptable in thy sight, O Lord, my strength, and my redeemer.

Psalm 19:14

206

As we live out this concept in our lives, we will discover it is not only the highest and healthiest way to live but also the most profitable.

14

Speak to the Dry Bones

The events of my life for the past few years remind me of a kaleidoscope. I entered a new world, my world view has changed, and for the first time in my life, I have new hope in my heart toward God's marvelous creation.

Just months ago, I could not have anticipated where my life has taken me or where my feet have walked. Helicopters, private jets, the White House, and steel plants never had been a part of my small world. I had thought in thousands of dollars, but now my mind could — for the first time — think about the possibility of the billions needed to revive a dying industry.

What Does It Mean To "Speak to the Dry Bones?"

But a thought still plagues me. Those words I heard on the bridge that day keep running through my mind: *Speak to the dry bones.*

Did I really hear from God? Is that Bethlehem Steel plant really "dead?" With the millions it would take to bring life back to that basic oxygen furnace, could it ever happen? *Speak life to dry bones.* What does it mean to me now?

As I ponder those words, I realize they are as alive in my spirit now as they were when I originally heard them in my heart. They still are as powerful and alive as the day I walked into Dr. Ken Lipke's office and attempted to tell him that I believed in his dream — or in fact, that it was our mutual dream. But now the voice seems even more distinct, more real, more vivid. This time, not for just one plant but for the American steel industry, the entire American industrial base.

I recall again my emotion-packed trip through the book of Daniel. I watched in awe as God pruned King Nebuchadnezzar's "tree."

I believe our entire industrial system today is going through a "pruning" designed by God. Without that pruning, we could not survive as an industrial nation. We have violated the principles of the Kingdom, and we need to accept the pruning process and the perfecting that it will bring.

The author of Hebrews wrote that Christ had been revealed in *the last days.* (Heb. 1:2.) *The last days* are not only those ahead of us, and eschatology is not just the study of the future. In a Biblical sense, *eschatology* is the study of the "last days," which began with the incarnation of Jesus and will culminate with the Second Coming.

The Day of the Return of the Servant-King

Satan's kingdom is made manifest in prejudice, hunger, poverty, crime, war, hatred, lack of commitment, sickness, and greed.

God's purpose in history is *victory over Satan through our Lord Jesus Christ.*

First John 3:8b says:

> **For this purpose the Son of God was manifested,
> that he might destroy the works of the devil.**

I believe that God made us instruments to enforce Satan's defeat in history and to enable Jesus Christ, the true ruler of history, to bless all the families of the earth, to "inherit the earth."

The foundation of this historic victory is not found in the future but in history, in the past.

Christ's person, work, and accomplishment of His first coming is the basis of our victory. The incarnation *was* the magnificent invasion of God into history. In that first coming, He not only took upon himself our sins, but He redeemed the earth. He judged the world system (the prince of this world was judged — John 12:31), became Lord of all, and created a new people who are the ongoing Kingdom. He established a victorious reign:

> **For he must reign, till he hath put all enemies
> under his feet.**
> **1 Corinthians 15:25**

It is this Church which must speak *spiritual life* into a decaying society. Our purpose is to enforce the victory Jesus won on the cross and to see that the redeemed earth is brought under subjection to the Lordship of Christ.

But how do we speak life to a decaying society? I believe we speak life in a number of ways into our society. Specifically, in those areas of business, we each can speak life according to the responsibility God has given us.

The *Christian worker* can speak life into the system by his very lifestyle. The way he works, the interest he shows in his job, the love he has for his company, the teamwork he shows, the lack of jealousy he shows to his employer — all *speak* life into a decaying system and bring renewal.

The *Christian manager* speaks life into decaying society through his very life system. We have gone to great lengths in this manuscript to speak life into a Christian management system. This system of servant-hood to supplier, employee, and customer is the very breath of life needed for a system that is now decaying.

The marvelous creativity of the entrepreneur will again speak life into our system. Consistently we hear of a call for entrepreneurship in America. Without the Holy Spirit and the creative ideas of God, that productive entrepreneurship is not available to the world. I believe that God right now is giving creative ideas to people across our world to serve as did Daniel in finding solutions to difficult problems.

How can I speak life into the dying steel industry? I do so by writing this book. The Biblical system contained in the pages of Holy Scripture has the very life needed for American industry. In these pages, we have tried to assemble that truth, that it may *speak life* into our system once again.

I am now far more excited than when I first traversed the Father Baker Bridge and heard those words in my spirit. Life is coming back to America. The absolutely phenomenal success of *In Search of Excellence* proves that America as the "pruned tree" is listening to the voice of the Spirit that is being heard throughout the land.

The day of the return of the servant-king is upon us once more. As Nehemiah rebuilt the walls of the city, we are today rebuilding the industrial walls of America.

I would challenge every pastor, every Sunday school teacher, every businessman who understands the principles that are contained in truth to articulate them to your world. We can all be a part together of *speaking life back to the system.*

Sources:
Additional Reading

Alderson, Wayne. *Stronger Than Steel*, Harper and Row, 1980.

Arnold, John D. and Tompkins, Bert. *How to Make the Right Decisions*, Mott Media, 1982.

Bluestone, Barry and Harrison, Bennett. *The Deindustrialization of America*, Basic Books, 1982.

Dunn, Samuel, compliler. *The Best of John Calvin*, Baker Book House, 1981.

Gibbs, Mark. *Christians With Secular Power*, Fortress Press, 1981.

Hybels, Bill. *Christians in the Marketplace*, Victor Books, 1982.

Johnson, Paul E. *A Shopkeeper's Millenium*, Hill and Wang, 1978.

Kuyper, Abraham. *Lectures on Calvinism*, William B. Eerdmans Publishing Company, 1931, 1983.

Lynd, Staughton. *The Fight Against the Shutdowns*, Singlejack, 1982.

Middelmann, Udo. *Proexistence*, Inter-Varsity Press, 1974.

Muller, Ronald E. *Revitalizing America: Politics for Prosperity*, Simon and Schuster, 1982.

Naisbitt, John. *Megatrends*, Warner, 1982, 1984.

Novak, Michael. *The Spirit of Democratic Capitalism*, Simon and Schuster, 1982.

Peters, Thomas J., and Waterman, Robert H., Jr. *In Search of Excellence*, Warner Books, 1984.

Schuller, Robert H. *Self-Esteem: The New Reformation*, Word Books Inc., 1982.

Toffler, Alvin. *Future Shock*, Bantam, 1971.

Toffler, Alvin. *The Third Wave*, Bantam, 1981.

Williamson, Peter, and Perrotta, Kevin, editors. *Christianity Confronts Modernity*, Servant Books, 1981.

For ministry information contact:

Tommy Reid
Full Gospel Tabernacle
P. O. Box 590
Orchard Park, New York 14127

*Please include your prayer requests
and comments when you write.*

Thomas F. "Tommy" Reid is pastor of the Full Gospel Tabernacle in Orchard Park, New York. He is a sought-after conference speaker, and his ministry touches the lives of thousands around the world.

For many years, Rev. Reid conducted evangelistic crusades with his father, the late Rev. Albert Reid, in many of the largest Assemblies of God churches and under gospel tents.

In 1959, he became pastor of Bethel Temple in Manila, the Philippines. The church was then known as the largest Protestant church in the Orient.

In 1963, Rev. Reid returned to America to assume the pastorate of a struggling church of less than one hundred people in Buffalo, New York. Full Gospel Tabernacle now has nearly five thousand people and a building complex valued at two million dollars. A major thrust of the ministry is planting new churches in the Buffalo area. One of them, New Covenant Tabernacle, has nearly two thousand members.

Rev. Reid is founder and president of Buffalo School of the Bible, an outreach of Full Gospel Tabernacle to train and equip lay leadership for ministry. He also is founder and president of the Association of Church-Centered Bible Schools, an organization to help churches establish their own Bible schools for lay leaders. Other outreaches of the church include a weekly television program, *Changing Your World*, a day care center, and several full-time missionaries.

Rev. Reid serves on the board of directors of Church Growth International, founded by Dr. Paul Yonggi Cho, pastor of the world's largest church in Seoul, South Korea. He also serves on the executive committee of Church Growth, Inc., Dr. Cho's television ministry.

A member of the executive committee of the New York State Association of Evangelicals, Rev. Reid also is one of the founding trustees of Charismatic Bible Ministries under the leadership of Oral Roberts.

Oral Roberts University and the California School of Theology both have recognized Rev. Reid's leadership and faithfulness in ministry by awarding him honorary doctorates. He serves on the board of regents of Oral Roberts University.

Printed in the United States
42158LVS00002B/88-180